SMART
MONEY
KIDS

A Parent's Guide to Digital Finance Education

by

Björn Nübel

Copyright © 2025 by Björn Nübel
Ink Media Publishing
All rights reserved.

No portion of this book may be reproduced in any form without written permission from the publisher or author, except as permitted by U.S. copyright law.

To request permission, contact author@bjoernnuebel.com.

This publication is designed to provide accurate and authoritative information in regard to the subject matter covered. It is sold with the understanding that neither the author nor the publisher is engaged in rendering legal, investment, accounting or other professional services. While the publisher and author have used their best efforts in preparing this book, they make no representations or warranties with respect to the accuracy or completeness of the contents of this book and specifically disclaim any implied warranties of merchantability or fitness for a particular purpose. No warranty may be created or extended by sales representatives or written sales materials. The advice and strategies contained herein may not be suitable for your situation. You should consult with a professional when appropriate. Neither the publisher nor the author shall be liable for any loss of profit or any other commercial damages, including but not limited to special, incidental, consequential, personal, or other damages.

ISBN: 978-1-964984-12-4 (Paperback)
ISBN: 978-1-964984-13-1 (eBook)

WHY YOU SHOULD READ THIS BOOK

Children growing up today have early contact with the digital world. Around 97% of all young people between the age of 14 and 19 have smartphones, use social media, and play online games.[1] As digital natives, they often move through the virtual world with greater ease and tend to know more – even than their parents – about various websites, how easy it is to purchase game and game credits with a debit/credit card, how to navigate Amazon and Netflix, and much more. However, they don't always know about the financial dangers the digital world holds, which creates a new challenge in their financial education.

This guide helps parents understand how cashless payments are changing consumer behavior and informs them of the traps that exist and await their children. This is particularly relevant as many providers use targeted psychological mechanisms to encourage spending.

Unfortunately, this isn't a topic that's taught in school. And the stakes are high. For example, when my friend's 12-year-old daughter got her first smartphone and began exploring online shopping, she was unaware of the financial consequences. She fell into the temptation of various deals. The app she used employed persuasive techniques, leading her to make impulsive purchases. Days later, my friend discovered a $500 charge and had to seek a refund. This incident emphasizes how easily children can be trapped by cashless systems. Parents must educate themselves and their children, discuss responsible spending, and be vigilant to protect their children's financial well-being in the digital age.

This book is also meant to help parents learn how to teach their children about financial literacy, including how to have money conversations with their children, what aspects of financial literacy should be discussed, and at what age.

The topic of financial literacy in children and young people is primarily viewed and presented on the web and by actors with specific interests, such as banks, financial service providers, and insurance companies. Driven by profit motives, these institutions present financial literacy in a way that favors their products and services. This bias can lead to a narrow understanding of financial concepts, potentially excluding important aspects such as saving, investing, and budgeting. It is crucial that your child receives a balanced and comprehensive financial education from independent sources to make informed decisions. There has been no transparent source that unites all sources and reduces complexity. Until today.

This book reveals the digital traps that exist and how parents can teach their children how to avoid them. It covers various dedicated approaches for children at different ages with a specific plan and recommendations on how to specifically promote financial literacy, and how to help children develop financial literacy in a world that is decoupled from cash.

So, if you are a parent or grandparent with children aged 5 to 21 years, this book is for you. Sit back, and let's dive in.

ABOUT THE AUTHOR

Björn Nübel is a financial expert who completed his training as a banker over two decades ago. He studied banking and banking supervision in Germany, then business administration in Switzerland and Chile. He has worked in the financial industry for over 25 years.

As the father to a lovely daughter who is a digital native, he is aware of the challenges of the "brave new world," and: this topic is particularly close to his heart. His approach to financial literacy is that the earlier you teach children how to handle money, the more successful they will be with it in the future.

In addition to his work as an author, Björn runs a blog focused on financial literacy for children at www.nuebel.blog, where he shares tips and insights for parents and educators. He also works as a freelance text coach, helping others communicate their ideas effectively at www.textcoa.ch.

TABLE OF CONTENTS

Why you should read this book 4

About the author 6

INTRODUCTION 11

    Why you should make your children money masterminds 13

MONEY TALKS 25

    Never too young 27

    Some examples: How to answer your children's questions 33

    Pitfalls you need to recognize when teaching children financial literacy 45

    The best time to have money talks with your children 55

    Having the conversation: Why talking about money matters 64

    Recap 65

EARNING 67

    Money as a tool for exchange 70

    Teaching Children about earning and the ATM 71

    Money, Survival, and the Principle of Exchange 78

    Important earning and investment lessons 85

    Earning for preteens (ages 9 to 12) 91

    Things to consider when making earning decisions for teenagers (ages 13 to 17) 95

    Recap 100

ALLOWANCES 103

Types of Allowances 109

Should you give your children (ages 5 to 8) an allowance?........ 112

How much allowance should you give your preteens
(ages 9 to 12)? 113

How much allowance should you give teenagers
(ages 13 to 17)? 115

Young adults (ages 18 to 21)... 115

Recap.. 118

SAVING & INVESTING 121

Emergency funds 125

How much should your children save? 127

Investing... 130

Saving goals for kids (ages 5 to 8) 132

How to help preteens (ages 9 to 12) start saving and investing.. 135

Practical steps to teach your teenagers (ages 13 to 17) saving
and investing.. 141

Steps on how young adults (ages 18 to 21) can start building
wealth... 152

Invest like a pro: the cost-average effect 154

Recap.. 156

SPENDING & DEBT 159

Practice budgeting for the future.. 184

How we can help our children build a good credit score from
an early age through credit cards 187

Recap.. 189

8

GIVING BACK & ENTREPRENEURSHIP 191
    How do you teach them to give at different ages? 193
    Safeguarding the next generation through financial literacy 195
    Entrepreneurship 200
    Recap 205

DIGITAL TRAPS: ENLIGHTENING YOUR CHILDREN 207
    Advertisers' traps 208
    Gaming traps 211
    Recap 227

CONCLUSION 229
    LITERATURE 232
    REFERENCES 235

INTRODUCTION

The National Teach Children to Save Day[2] is held in the United States of America each April to encourage children to develop good saving habits.

The event aims to teach children of different ages to become smarter with money and their finances. As financial literacy is arguably a more important subject than many taught in school, this event makes a good effort towards raising financially intelligent children.

But, even then, statistics from a 2019 National Foundation for Credit Counseling survey show how far we have come and how far we still are from attaining a 100% financial literacy rate in children of all ages. According to that piece of research, only 55% of adults give themselves an A or B when grading their knowledge of personal finance.[3] And slightly less than 25% of high school students took a personal finance course before graduating in 2022.[4]

If you ask me, we are far from proficient. This is partially because adults themselves may not have good financial habits, which makes it even more difficult to pass good habits on to their children. In fact, this makes the need to teach financial literacy from childhood even more urgent.

INTRODUCTION

WHY YOU SHOULD MAKE YOUR CHILDREN MONEY MASTERMINDS

If you are reading this book, it probably means that you consider financial literacy important for children. While reading this book you will learn:

- How to have money conversations with children, and;
- What aspects of money should be discussed, and at what ages.

The digital age started in the '60s and as we have progressed into the bittersweet years of the internet (bittersweet because, as advantageous as it is, there are some pitfalls), we see that this age is bound to last. Thanks to e-commerce and online payments, we're seeing drastic reductions in financial transactions using cash across various countries, with numbers decreasing every year. In a country like Sweden, for example, cash now accounts for only 2% of the total payments in the country. Many shops, cafés, and market stalls only accept cards, even for small amounts.

Gone will be the days where kids stockpile dollars in their piggy banks to watch their money physically grow. But the question is, as we move towards cashless societies, how can kids appreciate the value of money when money becomes a virtual concept and nothing physical is exchanged?

EVOLUTION OF
DIGITAL PAYMENTS

1960s

Introduction of credit cards
(e.g., Diners Club, American Express).

1980s

Emergence of Automated Teller Machines
(ATMs) and early online banking.

1990s

The Internet Era

1994: Introduction of online banking services
1998: Launch of PayPal, pioneering online payment services

2000s

Mobile and Online Expansion

2007: Launch of M-Pesa in Kenya, a mobile money service transforming payments in Africa
2008: Introduction of Bitcoin, sparking interest in cryptocurrencies

2010s

Rapid Growth and Innovation

2011: Launch of Apple Pay and Google Wallet, promoting mobile payments in the US and beyond
2015: India's demonetization, boosting digital payments through initiatives like UPI (Unified Payments Interface)

2020s

Mainstream Adoption and Future Trends

2020: COVID-19 accelerates contactless payments worldwide
2022: Central Bank Digital Currencies being explored by various countries

INTRODUCTION

Technology has been on a journey of continuous progression, evolving to meet the needs of billions of users. Many financial ideas and goals that were considered impossible centuries ago have been achieved and surpassed in the current digital age. One prime example is the widespread adoption and success of cryptocurrencies like Bitcoin. Centuries ago, the concept of a decentralized digital currency existing outside the control of any central authority would have been unthinkable. However, in 2009, Bitcoin was introduced as the world's first cryptocurrency, and it has since revolutionized the financial landscape.

Teaching kids about money has become more and more of a challenge for modern-day parents, due to the rise of the cashless economy, with the nature of virtual money making it difficult for children to know the consequences of overspending. And as there's limited cash to see or touch, there's little room to grasp the concept of saving.

As technology kept evolving according to the needs of the end-users, it became a necessity in the finance sector. Payments, standing orders, and share purchases are now made using smartphones and mobile banking apps, 24/7 and from any place on earth.

As of today, there are no completely cashless societies, but countries around the world are increasingly adopting cashless payment systems. Although a transition into full cashless economies is bound to happen someday, no one is sure of the exact time it will happen. According to various publications, Sweden was close to becoming a cashless society by 2023.[5]

Only 2% of the country's transactions are made in cash and 85% of people have access to online banking, according to the Consumer News and Business Channel (CNBC).[6]

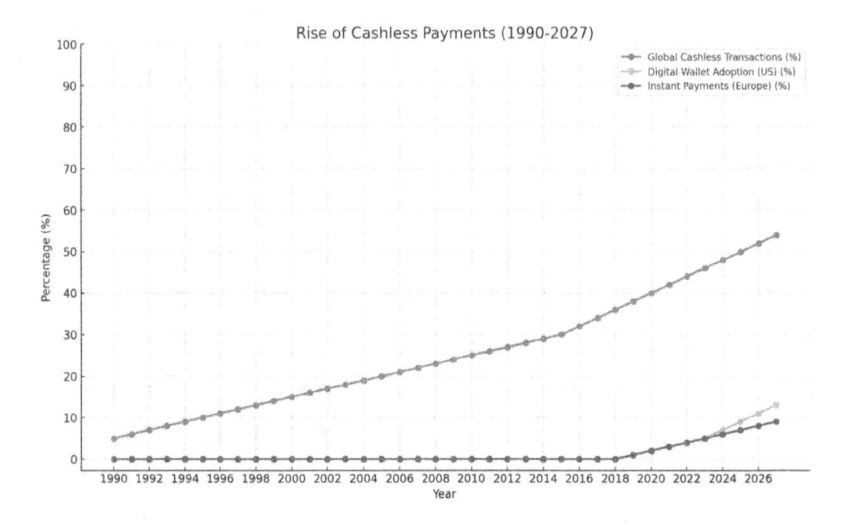

Rise of Cashless Payments (1990-2027)

— Global Cashless Transactions (%)
— Digital Wallet Adoption (US) (%)
— Instant Payments (Europe) (%)

This cashless movement is based on several different factors. The fact that most retailers in Sweden do not take cash purchases is, by far, the most powerful motivator. COVID-19 sped up cashless payment adoption in Sweden, as retailers preferred digital transactions, popular payment apps like Swish (a payment app in Sweden that is used by more than half of the population) reduced cash usage, and concerns arose regarding financial inclusion, privacy, and data security. Cash accounts for barely 20% of all in-store transactions in Sweden.

Funnily enough, I often see just the opposite in Germany—stores advertise that they now accept card payments. I assume that cultural differences and historical payment preferences – triggered by the experiences during and after the second world war – have led to Germany's reliance on cash, and thus resulting in slower adoption of card payments. However, increasing demand for convenience and the COVID-19 pandemic have accelerated the acceptance of card payments.

Currently, in the U.K., public transport no longer accepts cash, and the number of cashless payments such as credit cards, online payments, etc. are at an all-time high. Even the number of ATMs is gradually reducing. The U.K. is one of the leading regions in cashless payment adoption around the world today.

In 2021, Mastercard discovered a 97% rise in contactless payments across all of Europe.[7] However, during the COVID-19 pandemic, the trend toward contactless payment accelerated exponentially in many countries, primarily due to e-commerce and sanitation concerns.[8]

The more we think about it, the more obvious it appears that this trend will continue. Children from all over the world are growing up in this new reality. That is why it is critical that we prepare for this new reality and know exactly how to deal with it.

The Rise of Digitally Native Children

The number of children with access to the Internet at home via a range of digital devices has been steadily increasing in countries that are part of the Organization for Economic Cooperation and Development (OECD). From 2006 to 2015, the proportion of 15-year-olds in OECD countries with access to the Internet at home increased from 75% to 95%. Similar results were seen in the European Union (EU), with a rise in Internet access from 65% in 2011 to 90% in 2021. This ranged from 99% of households with Internet access in Luxembourg or the Netherlands to 84% in Bulgaria, the EU Member State with the lowest rate of Internet access. Households with children were more likely to have Internet access than those that did not (96% versus 82%).[9]

Other remarkable increases in access to technologies are evident. Computers used to be the device of choice for young people to access the Internet. However, over time, the popularity of mobile devices, such as tablets and smartphones, has exceeded that of computers. In 2015, 60% of children aged 15 reportedly used a desktop computer at least twice a week, while 91% of them owned or operated a smartphone daily. Additionally, 74% had access to a laptop and 53% always accessed the internet through a tablet (PISA 2015 report).[10] In a sample of preschoolers in the United Kingdom, parents reported that their children had access to an array of technological devices. 50% of the sample had access to between 4 and 10 devices, 32% had access to 11-20 devices, while 9% reported access to over 20 devices.[11] Devices included everything from smartphones to tablets to televisions. Despite progress in many OECD countries, it is crucial to emphasize that Internet use is less widespread in many countries outside of the OECD.[12]

Children were once referred to as "digital natives" in the literature, implying that because they grew up surrounded by technology and gadgets, they would know how to utilize them. But is that really the case? We'll look deeper at this concept in the next chapter.

Digital Immigrants and Digital Natives

The phrase "digital immigrant" refers to those who were born before the introduction of digital technology and were not exposed to it at a young age. Digital natives are the opposite of digital immigrants in that they have grown up with technology. Digital natives are a generation of young people who are "native speakers" of the digital language of computers, video games, and the Internet. However, this definition is highly critiqued. The ability or skill and tools required to go online don't necessarily make children savvy users, nor does it guarantee their online safety. The importance of introducing and instilling Information and Communications Technology (ICT) skills in younger children is being recognized by educational systems, as evidenced by a sharp rise in the integration of ICT into pre-primary curriculum frameworks across a number of jurisdictions in recent years.[13]

The following overview is based on the International Telecommunication Union's *Measuring the Information Society Report*[14] and an OC&C Strategy Consultants Study on Generation Z.[15]

SMART MONEY KIDS

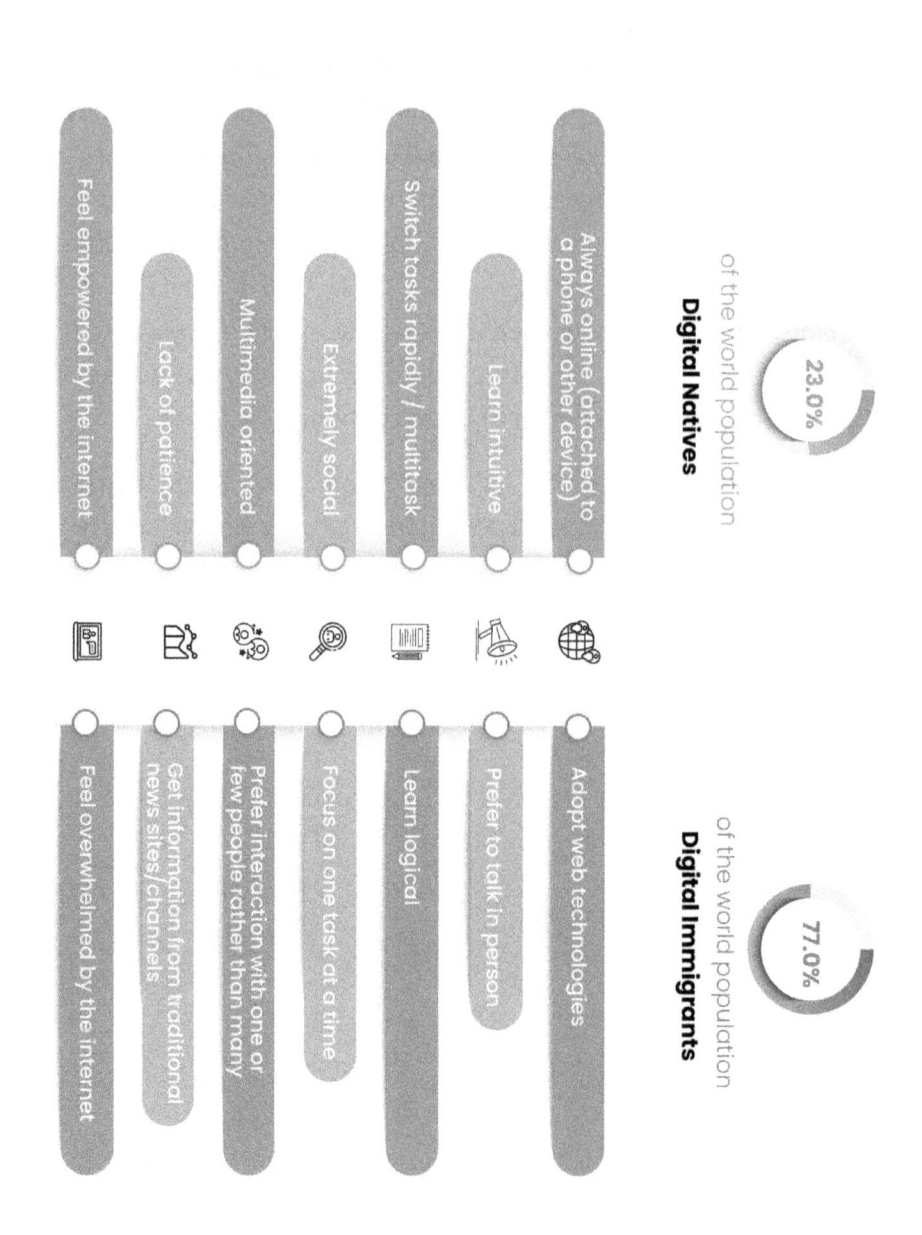

Digital Natives — 23.0% of the world population

- Feel empowered by the internet
- Lack of patience
- Multimedia oriented
- Extremely social
- Switch tasks rapidly / multitask
- Learn intuitive
- Always online (attached to a phone or other device)

Digital Immigrants — 77.0% of the world population

- Feel overwhelmed by the internet
- Get information from traditional news sites/channels
- Prefer interaction with one or few people rather than many
- Focus on one task at a time
- Learn logical
- Prefer to talk in person
- Adopt web technologies

Digital natives' need for financial literacy to survive in the rapidly developing digital world

Young children access the internet through a variety of devices and for a variety of reasons. The majority (73%) of parents with children aged 0 to 4 years old said that their children used a tablet to go online in the previous month. Meanwhile, 41% of respondents said their children used a smartphone or a mobile device, and 24% said they used a laptop or desktop computer.[16] In another survey of Estonian parents with children aged 0 to 3, it was found that children used communication tools such as FaceTime and Skype to communicate with close relatives, along with taking time to look at pictures. 25% watched TV, movies, and cartoons on their smartphones and tablets every day. Young children prefer touchscreen devices; tablets are popular in this generation because of their portability, screen size, and ease of use of the interface.[17] (I can confirm this from my own experience. A tablet or a smartphone magically attracts my daughter.)

One common risk in the widespread use of technology at a young age is that too many children use apps that are not appropriate for their age group.[18] Access to world of apps only underscores that parents should take great care to monitor their child's digital activity to ensure that materials are age-appropriate. Furthermore, instilling digital skills in children at an early age is critical so that they can utilize technology successfully and safely. We can even see basic digital literacy in children of young ages. 65% of children aged 0 to 5 years in the UK were able to swipe the screen without assistance, and 60% could trace shapes with their fingers and drag items around the screen. Only 14% of parents were able to acquire new apps in an app store/marketplace without assistance, with 61% unable or unaware of how to do so.[19]

That's just the 0-to-5-year range – can you imagine what children aged 5 to 15 years can do?

I am sure you're thinking about that already.

This highlights the need for children to learn about money; they need to know about earnings, bills and how they are paid, and many other money-related things. Imparting this knowledge ensures that parents raise children who are not afraid to discuss money or how to use money the right way.

The risk of cashless payment on "financially illiterate" children

The tap-and-go payment methods that are becoming increasingly popular in cashless economies make it easier than ever for our children to incur debt. A significant percentage of children (and their parents) are exposed to various debt traps since credit cards are now available to most of them.

The chief executive of non-profit Financial Basics Foundation, Katrina Birch, said in their latest survey of 1,100 Australian high school students that most respondents were confused about credit cards. Over half of these students thought they could pay off a $2,000 credit card debt in less than three years if they were paying the minimum amount of $41 (decreasing) per month at an 18% interest rate.[20]

The correct answer is 15 years.

Topics like financial literacy are not addressed the way they should be. Hence, the economic transition into a cashless world has a huge impact on our future generations. Given the complexities of both virtual and physical cash, it is essential that parents provide a comprehensive financial education to their children. My personal research, involving conversations with children of various ages, reveals diverse perceptions of money.

Personal research on the need for financial literacy in children

Children must learn these things whether they have contact with physical money or spend it online.

Teaching children about money is a way of protecting them. Making them financially aware from a young age puts them in a position to make better decisions about their money. Just remember that the consequences of debt can be detrimental, leading to financial stress and limitations in the future. Parents who are in debt can still break the cycle by teaching their children about responsible financial practices, empowering them to avoid accumulating debt as they grow up.

While working on this book, I spoke to children of different ages. I asked them what money is. They all gave various meanings, and lovely responses too. The four most common responses I received are listed below:

- Most children around age 5 said a variation of "Money is what mommy uses to buy nice things for us." "Especially my dolls," one of them added.
- Most children aged 9-10 said: "Money is used for paying bills and buying stuff."
- Children aged 12-13 said: "With money, we can change the world."

- Kids around the age of 15 described money as a tool for exchange, adding that they could get anything with money.

Brilliant answers, aren't they?

The single fact is that these children all know *something* about money, just like billions of other people in the world. But do they know **ABOUT** money? I don't want you getting confused here, but as an adult/parent we know that knowing how to spend money is only a part of the money equation. Some could argue that how to spend money is the least important thing about money.

You'll notice that a good part of the answers was centered around where or how to spend money. This is not surprising, because in most instances the aspect of money we allow children to see are the parts that involve spending it. Now, with the digitalization of finance, many children do not even get to witness as much as they should when it comes to our spending habits.

This book gives you an actionable guide to help your children to learn about the many aspects of handling and talking about money in a digital world. It helps you to successfully incorporate money lessons into the daily routines and lives of your children. (Even better, many parents will learn something, too.)

So, what are you waiting for? Let's get started!

MONEY TALKS

People are more comfortable talking about almost everything else more than money. Adults often confess that they would prefer having a conversation about sex with children (which has been widely considered a difficult and uncomfortable topic) rather than a money talk, especially specifics. For example, they may talk about getting a raise but be uncomfortable about mentioning how much of a raise they got.

Over the years, money has become an issue around which most people tiptoe. When you address the matter head-on, you can often be considered daring, bold, or sometimes downright rude. This is an appalling situation, to say the least.

The cultural taboo around discussing money has developed for several reasons. Though these reasons differ from person to person, the underlying consensus is that people find it awkward.

I read a discussion on an internet forum about finance months ago. A woman was invited to hang out with a few friends and the discussion was steered towards their careers. She asked one of her acquaintances how much she earned at her new job. The looks she got in return spoke volumes, something along the lines of "How dare you ask me that!"

She did not see anything wrong with the question and was only asking because she was thinking of making a career change. Naturally, she wanted to know what she could expect to earn. The awkward silence she received from her peers was unexpected. Never once had she thought that asking a person what they earned was rude, especially when the information would be of practical help.

Her family was one where everyone had an idea of what their parents earned, as it allowed them to budget and make the most of the family's income. In her words, "That incident opened my eyes to the fact that not every family was like mine. I find it fascinating because this taboo appears to be the way of life for many."

Now, many people would think this taboo is limited to talking about salaries, but it is not. The common ground is *money*.

For most individuals, talking about money is a difficult topic since it triggers so many strong emotions—pride, shame, and envy, to mention a few. When it comes to discussing money with someone you love, it's even more difficult.

"Nobody's taught to talk about money, much less with our families," said certified financial planner Hannah Moore, in an interview for CNBC's American Greed.[21] Moore, the president of a Dallas-based firm, works with retirees and said conversations about money are key. "These conversations are difficult and awkward, but they're incredibly important."

Children raised in families who fail to have "the money conversation" may find themselves unable to satisfy basic requirements or unable to deal with the financial ups and downs that are a part of everyone's journey through life.

NEVER TOO YOUNG

"Next month, I'll have a three-year-old," Moore said. "There are appropriate money conversations for me to be having with her."

Help your children learn the basics of financial management by guiding them through your process of keeping track of your checking and savings accounts. Talk to them about your charitable contributions, too.

The primary focus should be on how to value and think about money. The significance of planning, saving, and patience may be taught to children by involving them in financial objectives like buying a new item at home or taking a trip.

"It's about passing down these values that families have," Moore concluded.

As kids grow older, you'll have discussions about college savings and how to budget for big life milestones. So, it's critical to understand what your family can afford, especially in this current age of heavy student debt and increasing tuition fees. You need to explain to your children how debt works, how there's always interest attached to debt, and that all this needs to be paid off.

There is no reason to stop there; continue until your children become adults.

As adults, many of our habits reflect the things we picked up from our parents or the adults in our lives. Our environment shapes us. It might not be intentional, but if we grow up in an environment where talking about money is considered taboo or uncomfortable, we will be conditioned to look at it that way. This can cause us to ignore serious financial red flags for fear of discussing them.

This is the risk faced by our children, especially in a digital world where they hardly see cash and everything happens online.

Without clear and consistent discussions about money, children will acquire their knowledge of money matters from random sources on the internet, all because the adults in their lives did not deem it fit or found it too uncomfortable to talk about.

According to a Chase Slate survey, only 56% of parents claim to have discussed money with their children.[22] And even then, T. Rowe Price, an independent investment management firm, found that 77% of parents only touch on the topic during a discussion about future careers. 73% believe it's important to include kids in discussions regarding the family finances.[23]

Most people tend to be shy or feel ashamed around money conversations, and some were taught things like "never count someone else's money"—an adage that can lead to good lessons, like not feeling jealous of another person. But this can also lead people to believe it's bad to even bring up money.

Of course, kids don't just learn from what parents tell them. They learn even more from what their parents do. So, we must walk the talk. Even though over 80% of the parents T. Rowe surveyed claimed they are setting a good example by having the money conversation, 40% still take the "do what I say, not what I do" approach.

It's also true that kids can, and should, learn about financial issues and topics in other ways, including at school. But the education of children is the responsibility of parents. According to the results of the Chase Slate survey, "Americans say they owe their financial foundation to their parents."

> *Parents at EVERY income level should make sure that their child receives a strong financial education!*
>
> *– Wakiti Muhammad*

The ideal question we should ask ourselves is: "Will this foundation be solid enough for the future?"

Learning about money from the internet without proper guidance is a debt trap that many parents allow their children to fall into. Why? Because most of this learning on the internet is about spending money.

You'll come across various topics like how to buy things from a local store without leaving your room, how to buy your favorite game now and pay later, and so on. There are just too many to mention them all, compared to content about how kids can save or invest money. It seems like everything we see online these days, even in an entertainment format, involves promo codes and opportunities to buy.

Most kids are not prepared to understand or engage with discussions about financial responsibility, such as saving or investing, because they lack awareness of these concepts and their significance. Thus, it's the parent's job to educate them on the topic, and most parents never tell children the importance of saving. Children are left believing that if they needed to save or invest, their parents would have mentioned it.

Where Did This Culture of Not Discussing Money Start?

Many people are told not to discuss money, but no one really knows where this trend originated. According to an article published by *Forbes* in 2015, our money taboo derives from the British. For Jodi R. R. Smith of Mannersmith Etiquette Consulting, the British have long considered it impolite to discuss money: "The affluent didn't need to talk about it because they already knew—from how many mansions you had, what vehicles you drove, how many maids you had, the ships you owned, and where you vacationed. They'd be able to figure out your net worth."[24]

However, the United States differs from the United Kingdom in one important way: It is significantly larger. "As a result, your net worth became little distinct from your capacity to buy property here," Smith explains, "since practically everyone could own property."

Still, it is considered impolite to discuss one's finances in old money circles, which is why someone with such a background could answer, hazily, "Yes, it was a nice year." People with new money, on the other hand, would feel more comfortable talking about figures like $3,000,000.

This cultural norm has been perpetuated over decades, with friends and family shying away from bringing up the topic at all. After all, little drops of water can eventually form an ocean.

If you are reading this book, it means you are willing to break the cycle and give your children the best financial education possible.

A survey conducted by Wells Fargo found that "71% of adults surveyed learned the importance of saving from their parents. Despite this, only a third (36%) of today's parents report discussing the importance of saving money with their children frequently, with 64% indicating they talk about savings with their kids less than weekly or never."[25]

So, do parents need to change and start discussing money and finance with their children? YES!

This change will not happen as fast as we want it to, but the rise in the amount and quality of resources to give children a sound financial education is a good sign.

A colleague once asked me: "Are children interested in learning about money and all of its complexities?" I thought this was a surprising question. Indeed, should we wait for our children to show interest in education before we sign them up for school? Of course not. If we keep looking for a sign before we take our children's financial literacy seriously, we may never broach the topic. Imagine if you waited to teach your child how to read until the child seemed interested in reading. How behind would they be?

It's also common for adults to miss out on opportunities to discuss the issue altogether. Here are ways that children often ask about money that you may have overlooked, which are all openings to discuss money with them.

When children ask questions like:

- Are we rich or poor?
- Why can't I have a card to buy whatever I want?
- Can I go to the ATM and just get money?
- Why don't we have a house like Karl's?
- Ben's family is going on vacation, can we go too?
- Can we eat out today?
- How much do you make?

These are signs you are not having the money talk with them, and at the same time, they are openings to start a conversation on the topic.

The above illustrates just a few examples. There are many other questions children ask that may be your chance to turn a simple inquiry into a teachable moment and ongoing conversation.

It is important to note that answering many of these questions is not always straightforward. You might not be able to give your children your personal financial information, but you can explain to them what money is, how it's being used, and most importantly how to use it the right way. Answering questions smartly and sharing knowledge is important.

So that's why we'll be looking at some of them in the next chapter.

SOME EXAMPLES: HOW TO ANSWER YOUR CHILDREN'S QUESTIONS

Are We Rich or Poor?

It's natural for young kids to start wondering about their financial standing. As early as age four or five, some children want to know where their family stands. It is natural to compare ourselves to what we see around us, and socioeconomic disparities are not lost even on small children. They usually tend to think about it in black or white terms. That is, they are either 'rich' or 'poor,' compared to other people they know or see in movies. This is not just a teachable moment for the children but also a moment that can shape how they perceive the world. You can teach them that being rich is relative. That being rich isn't only measured in financial terms, or that even if somebody seems to have or spend more money than others that doesn't necessarily mean they are rich.

The data reveals that the main characteristic that differentiates the wealthy from the poor is their dedication to saving money. Yes, this statement is very general, and it completely ignores the difficult financial situations in which many families find themselves. However, researchers found that "higher lifetime income households save a larger fraction of their income than lower-income households."[26]

Hence, those who have a lot of money tend to save a lot of money. Just knowing that is worth its weight in gold because you can use this knowledge for yourself. Now I will show you why.

For most people, spending comes before saving. Only what's left afterward is saved. With that in mind, let's imagine a family makes a total of $2,500 each month, and they are only left with $125 to save after settling their necessities and a few extras.

When all is said and done, they end up saving only 5% of their monthly income. Unfortunately, unforeseen circumstances or expenses are bound to come up, which can easily consume that 5%. Some families see the leftovers as so small that they don't even make an effort to save it.

The situation is vastly different among the rich, who often save 30%, 40%, or even 50% of their salary, even when financial advisors recommend saving and investing 10% or 15% of their monthly income.

No doubt saving that much money can only be achieved if you are living below your means. The more money you save and invest, the higher the income you can earn from it.

A small example will help you to understand the context better: Let's take the hypothetical family with a $2,500 monthly income we discussed before. In this case, the only difference is that this family saves and invests $125 per month. With an average yearly return on a portfolio that might include stocks and bonds but focuses on equities (often 8% return is assumed here on average), the family could expect nothing less than $71,617.47 in 20 years. Of course, there are bull (persistently rising stock prices) and bear (persistently falling stock prices) markets, but empirical data proves that markets move upwards in the long term. The good news is that if you save money that you don't have to rely on, you won't be forced to liquidate investments if the markets don't perform well.

Let's look back at our example. Within the next 20 years, the family won't be billionaires, but their wealth will likely reach $405,423.43 if they keep saving $125 each month. Even that tiny 5% will compound over the years, making it not so small after all.

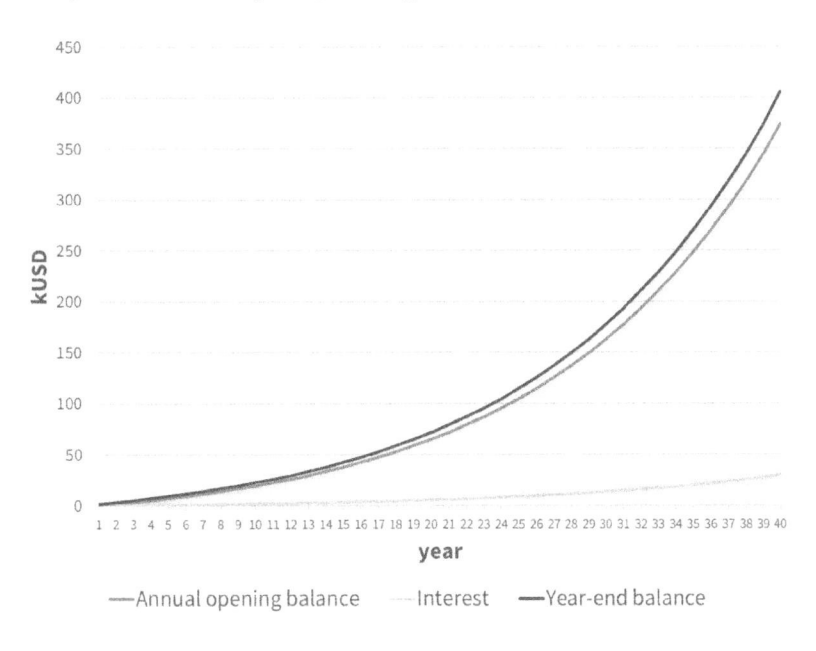

Wealth growth ($125 monthly additions over 40 years)

When you invest, it compounds over time. Your money will start making money. That's why saving money is more important than earning more money in the long run. Ultimately, it is saving and investing that makes people rich and encourages financial freedom. Having money to spend just means you are working and making money, but it doesn't mean you are rich.

I'm sure you're now wondering, "How do I explain this to my kids?" I don't want to reveal too much at this point (No, I don't keep any secrets), but one thing is clear: You will find the answer in this book.

The answer of being rich or poor is not solely about how much money your family has. Wealth is relative and can be influenced by factors such as saving money and making wise financial choices.

So, instead of labeling ourselves as rich or poor, let's focus on understanding the value of saving and investing. By making smart financial decisions and saving even a small amount consistently, we can build wealth and improve our financial situation over time. It's not about how much money we have right now, but rather about developing good habits and planning for the future. Remember, being rich isn't just about having a lot of money. It's about having financial stability and the freedom to make choices that are important to us.

But Mom, Why Can't I Have a Credit Card?

Depending on their age and concept of money, some kids don't understand that credit or debit cards don't represent endless supplies of money. Children tend to ask this question when they witness adults pull out their cards to pay for groceries. Let's face it, it is a valid question! Why can't they?

You can tell them that they can one day have a card, however, it will come to them when they have the responsibility to use it. You can refer to something that they are responsible for, no matter how small, to put this into perspective—like their piggy bank—so they know that they can only have it when they are ready for the responsibilities that come with it, not just to buy anything they like.

Also, explain that what is contained within the card is actual money and they would need to have their own money to own a card. This may be a great opportunity to discuss spending versus saving, and assets versus debts.

In terms of buying whatever they want, you can teach them that most people who use their cards to buy what they want can do that because they've taken time to learn how to make money and manage their budget. Therefore, they know that if they buy something, it's not going to affect their financial status or budget goals.

Can I Go to the ATM and Just Get Money?

It is not news that many children think that their parents have a storeroom filled with money because they just seem to magically bring it out when it is needed. But children must understand that money does not just spring out of the ATM. Explain that an ATM is like their savings. Use the example of a piggy bank if they have one. In fact, I recommend encouraging your child to keep a piggy bank so they can start visualizing money from an early age. Explain that if they do not put money in their piggy banks, they will not have money to take out of it when they need it. (And usually, money is earned with hard work.) The money in the piggy bank is limited to the amount they have kept in it, and that is how using an ATM works. You cannot go and take out what you have not kept there.

Why Don't We Have a House Like Karl's?

When children make comparisons, parents have a good opportunity to discuss prioritization. What Karl's family likes or wants or can afford is not what others like or want or can afford. Give examples with items your children own or want to own and let them know to weigh needs and affordability carefully. Just like they might want something and not be able to afford it, tell them that's one of the reasons they should start saving. This will help them make the connection that saving early can help them afford what they want.

Can We Eat Out Today?

If you don't have the money, be honest. Tell them you must use the money for something else (name the thing) and that you are cutting down on the family's expenditures so that your finances can accommodate a bigger or more important expense.

If you have the money and you are only trying to teach them how to budget or manage finances, be honest about that too. Explain to your child that just because you have the means to do something doesn't automatically mean you need to or should.

Let them know the difference between necessity and want. They need to know that some things will not change them or their situation while others will do just that.

How Much Money Do You Make?

You do not necessarily need to disclose an income number to answer this question. Some children, maybe aged 5-11, might not be mature enough to handle the details and may feel the need to compare with other children. In many cases, younger children may not be able to grasp the difference between a salary of $100 and $1,000, just like older children might have the same issues with $10,000 and $100,000. (Recently, my daughter said to me: "This [a children's book] must be expensive. It's definitely two hundred million thousand." I bet you know these situations, too.)

So, do not feel the need to throw specific figures at them. Instead, use this as an opportunity to teach your children what your salary can cover—items like the family's housing, food, utility bills, and possibly healthcare and other things. Use this as a chance to explain where budgeting and saving come in. Let them know that, even if you can afford what the family needs in a particular month, you may not be able to afford it the following month if the family expenses keep growing.

You can opt to make it a fun money lesson. Using play money, show them how your earnings take care of the family expenses, show them how you take a certain sum for food expenses, utility bills, and other expenses that your earnings can cover. Also, don't forget to mention the ones you couldn't cover and tell them that it may escalate more if they don't learn to manage the family's budget and money the right way.

Why Are Money Talks Important?

Teaching your children about money is no different from the myriads of things they must learn before they can be capable adults. Hence, conversations about money with your children are fundamentally different than those you would have with adults.

I am convinced that you want your children to have a healthy relationship with money. The same goes for having healthy conversations about money with other people; it is only good that you teach your children to do the same.

First, I will address the common mistake many parents make, which is that they only talk to their children about money when they start having a financial crisis. Or that they only have money discussions that come from stress or frustration. You don't want your child to learn about money by overhearing financially based arguments between you and your spouse.

You being proactive about financial conversations will help them have a better perspective through both good and challenging financial times. If they don't value or appreciate where the money comes from, they will have difficulties accepting changes when the situation calls for it. This is a good time to pause and reflect. Ask yourself, what were the "money stories" you heard during childhood? Dive deep into those memories and discover how they shaped your beliefs and behaviors around finances.

Let us look at the "why."

Why should your children be financially literate?

- *It prepares them*: The earlier we teach children that life can deal us many different hands, the better for them. Many life and relationship issues stem from money. Just because children don't know about certain financial situations does not prevent them from facing them later. Situations like loss of employment and bad business deals happen. Saving to buy a house, start a business, or even just ensure you have enough money to live and fulfill your obligations are all situations we should be prepared for. Teaching children about emergency funds and why they are important may save them in the future.

Learning about money through experiences with external sources, like when they start making purchases online, will only give them a one-sided view of what money is about, which is the spending aspect, and that does not prepare them for what they will face later.

- *It gives them the confidence to talk about money which ultimately gives them freedom in that sphere of their life:* If left unchecked, the cycle of avoiding the money topic can be passed on from generation to generation. For example, let's say that Mr. A, a civil engineer, got married to a data analyst. They are both successful in their respective fields. A few years later, they have a daughter named Isabel. They are amazing parents who dote on their child, providing everything Isabel needs and almost everything she wants. Isabel grows up thinking her parents are rich, not because they told her this, but because compared to her friends, she has "everything." The fact that all her friends say that her parents are 'money bags' also drove that point home for her. She does not know the reasons behind her mother's sacrifice. In fact, her mother stopped her monthly personal shopping to set money aside for housing bills. However, her parents told her that mom just got bored with shopping and it was something that commonly happened to adults. This did not matter to her, because they bought her the set of kicks she wanted that same week. Meanwhile, her friend at school had to change schools because his father lost his job. She went home and asked her parents if they could ever find themselves in that position, and they told her an emphatic "no." This reassured her that her parents had enough money, and they would never be in that position. And yet, this was not true. Isabel's parents had faced financial hardships, even if she hadn't had to change schools. Isabel only found out about most of this when she became an adult, realizing then that her parents were not as rich as she had thought. As an adult, Isabel started her own family, and the cycle continued. Because she came from a family where money talks hardly occurred, it was difficult for her to talk about it with her own family when she finally became a parent herself. This worsened since her spouse happened to be brought up in a similar environment where having such conversations was taboo.

That's one major reason we have children who cannot comfortably have conversations about money today: They learn their behavior from their parents. Of course, there are exceptions, but in a lot of cases that is what happens. Teaching your children about money is the best way to build their confidence and allow them to have healthy conversations about money, rather than trying to shield them from it or letting them learn about it unsupervised over the internet or through modern culture (what they see on TV, in movies, from people they admire like pop icons, etc.). It is crucial to be able to talk about money because it empowers children to understand and manage their finances effectively. Open discussions about money provide opportunities to learn about budgeting, saving, investing, and making informed financial decisions, leading to greater financial literacy and confidence in navigating the complexities of the modern financial world.

- *It alleviates their concerns:* Parents sometimes think that hiding the truth from their children is a way of protecting them. This is not always true, especially when it comes to money. Children are observant and can often soak up conversations that happen in the household. They might not fully understand them, or they might only hear parts of the conversation and draw their conclusions. This runs the risk of them drawing the wrong conclusions or magnifying the problem, in turn causing them stress.

  If there are money issues that require a change in the family's lifestyle or an adjustment in the household, then you must be honest with children about it and point out what changes need to be made and how long they might last. This prepares them and takes away the stress of second-guessing, and possibly imagining something much worse.

- *It relieves your stress:* I spoke to a parent who said he had not realized how wound up he was about his financial state, how it affected his children, and the whole process of keeping it from them until he opened up about it. In his words, "It was like I could finally breathe, and I did not even know I was holding my breath."

  Concealing a financial hardship winds up being more stressful for everyone involved. Being honest is not only a relief for you because you no longer must keep up the charade, but it will help your child gain perspective. This is especially true when you go through a financial crisis or when your children make a poor decision with money. However, this doesn't mean you should burden them with all the details of your financial issues, as this could affect them mentally, too. You just need to talk to them about the parts that affect them.

Just think about it, does the idea of having financially educated children not make you breathe more freely? Is it not relaxing to think that, even when you do not have any financial setbacks that may require a change of lifestyle for your children, you can rest assured that they know what they need to know about money? I think it is extremely comforting, especially in our current economy, marked with enough uncertainties to go around.

- *It allows you to talk about mistakes:* When adults admit their own mistakes, it helps children have more understanding and perspective around their own inevitable mistakes. Most adults have made mistakes that they could have avoided if they'd been knowledgeable about money. Help your children avoid those same mistakes by talking about them openly. You can even discuss possible or "near mistakes" and the consequences of what could have happened. If you feel children learn things faster while having fun, make it fun. Teach them with money cards if you think it might help, but don't let it detract from the seriousness of the topic. When you are intentional about their financial literacy, it opens a platform to infuse lessons from your own money mistakes.

PITFALLS YOU NEED TO RECOGNIZE WHEN TEACHING CHILDREN FINANCIAL LITERACY

There are several pitfalls when it comes to teaching financial literacy to children.

Leaving children to their own devices

Many parents make the mistake of thinking their children will eventually learn all there is to know about money on their own. This is especially true of parents with good money habits. They assume the child will learn by example. However, while your child is more likely to have good financial habits because you do, leading by silent example is not good enough. Something so important deserves to be actively taught. Learning about the intricacies of money requires discipline. Have you ever met a disciplined person who became disciplined without being intentional? I haven't. Leaving children to their own devices does not instill in them the discipline that managing money requires.

What would you do if you had the option of saving or spending money for the rest of your life with no consequences? I, without hesitation, would choose to spend, as would most people. Spending is naturally more fun because it requires no discipline and satisfies our desire for instant gratification. During my apprenticeship as a banker, I read the following saying at the bank's headquarters: "*Spare wenn du hast, damit du hast in der Not,*" which translates as: "Save when you have money, so you have money when in need."

If you, as an adult, would choose spending over saving, it is not hard to figure out why your child would as well. Saving is essentially a form of delayed gratification. It is understandable why this may not be a preferred option for children, *especially* those who are on social media platforms that seem to become more buying-oriented every year. I think it is wishful thinking to believe that as children grow up, they will quickly realize the advantages of being financially responsible. In fact, most people's financial habits are established as early as when they are seven years old.[27] Letting your children navigate financial matters on their own increases the risk of them growing up with bad financial habits. This leaves them with the struggle of trying to break bad habits later in life or the struggle of living with bad money decisions and their consequences. It is easier to learn good habits than break bad ones, and it's up to parents to take the responsibility of educating their children financially.

Avoiding the topic

Discussing money should not be taboo. This cannot be said enough times.

You would be surprised (or not, as you may witness this every day) how much TV our children are exposed to and how many ads they see from the time they spend on TV in a day. Children aged 2 to 5 spent over 32 hours per week watching television. Kids aged 6 to 8 spent 28 hours per week in front of the screen.[28] A survey of children aged 8 to 18 by the KAISER FAMILY FOUNDATION found that watching television in different forms, including on mobile phones and the Internet, has risen to 4.5 hours every day for this age group.[29] Another survey done by COMMON SENSE MEDIA found that kids at the age of 8 and below spend an average of 2 hours and

19 minutes on-screen daily. TV and video accounts for 72% of that time, which is an all-time high since 2011 when the average daily screen time for the same age group was 1 hour and 55 minutes. Mobile phone usage has climbed dramatically since 2011, while time spent on other devices has decreased.[30] Where I'm leading with these worrying statistics is that you do not need to be a financial genius to know that the ads they are exposed to do not encourage anything else but mass consumption and instant gratification, which is bad for children's financial choices.

So, avoiding conversations about money with your children and relying on them educating themselves through unhealthy mediums should be avoided at all costs. As uncomfortable as it might be at first, parents must give it a shot and keep at it. If you are just starting to try to talk about money with your children, a good way to start is to find out what they already know. For instance, ask them: "Tell me about the best and worst things you've ever spent money on and how you felt afterwards."

I want to share with you a real-life example of how powerful TV commercials can be. It was during the pre-Christmas period of 2021 that we were guests of my parents-in-law in the south-eastern Alpine valley of Switzerland, near the Italian border.

Everything was perfect. Beautiful snow-capped mountains, the house heated by a warming fire from the fireplace, and everywhere it smelled like Christmas. (Yes, that sounds a bit cheesy. And it was.)

My daughter ran through the house and told everyone what gifts she wanted from Santa Claus. To me she said, "Daddy, I want a doll that can walk on its own and talk to me!" I liked the idea, but I knew that she wouldn't get that doll from Santa.

It was when we were watching cartoons in the afternoon and I saw a commercial that I understood why she wanted that doll. In a commercial there was a doll that walked and talked by itself. However, it was the ads that suggested this doll could do it. (Of course, she COULD NOT.)

I took this opportunity immediately and asked my daughter if it was the doll she had wanted. (Direct hit!) That's exactly what she was – the ultimate doll. The good thing about the situation, the doll was the sister model of an already beloved doll she owned. And that's exactly what I used to start the discussion.

I told her that the doll and Alice looked very alike and that the only difference seemed to be their hair. It took a moment, but she finally said that it must be Alice's sister. Yes, I agreed that made sense, but I also said that Alice couldn't walk on her own, nor did she talk. My daughter confirmed this with a laugh, saying "But Daddy, that's not possible." I then explained to her that it is important for her to understand that TV commercials only want her to buy a product. TV commercials show things that aren't real, that don't exist in the real world. I explained this was like the dogs from Paw Patrol, or are there real dogs that can talk? She understood that immediately. And the best part? She now asks me if certain things are "real" and that's detached from television. She understood the concept and applies it now to all other things (not only to TV commercials) to actively question whether things can be as they seem to be.

Did I choose the best approach to help her? To be honest, I don't know. But I know it worked for me.

Bribing them for things they should normally do

Offering pocket money for chores is a good way to teach your children financial responsibility and the art of negotiation. But paying them to do what they ought to be doing as a member of the household, e.g., doing the dishes, taking out the trash, or cleaning their own room, can be a disservice to them.

The amount a parent bribes their children to do a chore at age seven is likely to go up at age ten, and it will only keep rising from there. So, instead of starting something that you might not be able to sustain or may harm your children's relationship with money, create an allowance system that functions independently of the chores they should in any case be doing. This is a good lesson, both in terms of personal responsibility and managing finances.

Underestimating what they can understand

Never underestimate your children. Never!

Children are smarter than many of us believe. You may only be teaching them about spending and savings because you think that is all they can understand at their age, but children are naturally curious and fast learners. Why not teach them something beyond savings and spending, like investing?

You can introduce the concept to them, and they do not have to figure it all at once—some adults have not figured it out at all! — and it is alright to take it slow and teach them what you can. Investor Kevin O'Leary said he wanted his children to learn about investing, so he got them a transparent piggy bank. To teach them about compound interest, every time they put money into their piggy banks, he added pennies to the bank while they slept. This may seem like such a simple idea, but it's an effective one.

Introduce different aspects of finances to your children gradually. They do not have to learn all of it at once, but it will lay a good foundation to prepare them, and they will thank you for it later.

Taking control of all their spending

Compared to children, we, as adults, tend to feel like we know it all, or that we make the best decisions. Maybe sometimes we do, but when it comes to bringing up financially literate children, we must allow them a little freedom to make their own financial decisions and even mistakes. This isn't to say they should have all the freedom in the world, but they should have the opportunity to show you that they are learning or to help you see knowledge gaps that you can help fill.

Most parents lean towards one of two extremes: They either try to micromanage their children's every move or they neglect their parental duties completely. My view is that we shouldn't do either. We should let children make some decisions for themselves, letting them make mistakes and learn from them. You do not want to bring up a child who grows up to depend on you for every financial decision they make. Be there to guide them but avoid micromanaging them. Let them understand the consequences of their actions and give them the opportunity to be proud of their good decisions. Allowing them to experience the ups and downs of their financial decisions can be an effective way of teaching them the value of a dollar—and the benefits of making smart financial decisions.

Not letting them see you shop

It is unwise to equip your children with knowledge but not allow them to practice all they have learned. This is especially true in this digital and post-COVID-19 era, where the exchange of physical cash is not as common as it used to be. Many transactions are carried out online, including purchases, bills, payments, and a myriad of other financial transactions. You must teach your children not to only see the cashless side of financial transactions because it might give them a false idea of spending and money.

Though this may be considered old school now, you should take your children to a physical store and allow them to watch and participate in the shopping experience, witness you pay in cash, and get change. What also works very well is when your child is allowed to pay and receive the change on your behalf. The simple truth is that, as we move toward a cashless society, fewer children will have the important experience of actually handling physical money. I can still remember very clearly how my daughter came back to me with a beaming smile and full of pride with the appropriate change when she paid for me for the first time. "Dad, I always want to pay for you from now on," she said.

This simple act will do a few things for them: They will understand cost and value, and they will understand that money has an actual limit. Let them in on the shopping budget, so they can help with shopping decisions like selecting and comparing products on the shelf, putting into consideration cost and value based on the available budget. If you are deciding between the name-brand and generic version of toilet paper, walk them through why. Know that, for your children, even the littlest things count, and it is easy to turn every learning moment into a fun lesson.

Forcing saving on them

You might ask: How is this a mistake? As an adult who has either reaped great benefits from saving or who made the mistake of not saving and is bearing the brunt of it, it can be tempting to impose saving money on children.

Instead, help them see the importance of saving so that they are empowered to make the decision for themselves. One lifelong lesson I have learned is that demanding that your children save could do more harm than good to their financial habits. Because you can only force them for a period, eventually, when they are free to make their own decisions, they might just see it as a burden they need to drop, which is ultimately bad for their finances.

Do not force them, and be patient when you teach them. They need to see the benefits and do it of their own accord. Perhaps they save their birthday money this year but spend their Christmas money on a toy they really want. It's all about balance!

Try not to impose any financial habits on your children. Keep the relationship open, honest, and approachable.

Skipping credit and debt lessons

This subject should not be overlooked for any reason because the amount of people swimming in credit card debt is alarming. In a recent survey by Bankrate.com, 54% of adults were found to carry credit card balances over from one month to another, with 50% of these same adults having been in a credit card debt for at least 1 year.

For every person with credit card debt, the average debt owed is $5,525. If they only pay the minimum payment, with interest of over $6,000, it will take about 16 years before this debt could be paid.

This is a tricky subject for both children and their parents, especially if parents are struggling with credit card debt themselves. While preschoolers may not be able to grasp such concepts, you can begin discussing credit and debt with middle or high school aged children.

Unfortunately, many don't learn about debt until they're in it! Neglecting this topic means sending children to college and letting them face debt and credit card applications with no knowledge of them, which become increasingly common at that age. Without proper lessons, they will likely imitate their peers and sign up for credit cards, which risks leading them to confuse their new credit limit with actually having money. The simplest way to teach them about the effects of interest is to give them a small amount of money and give them a deadline to repay you with interest.

Let say your child wants to get a box of LEGOs for $20. All you must do is agree to lend them the $20 on credit if they agree to pay it back with an interest of maybe $5. So, by doing this, they will learn the fact that getting money quickly on credit/loan comes with interest, so they should only go for it if it's really necessary.

Missing the lesson on generosity

Missing this topic is usually not intentional; some parents just do not consider it an important money lesson. The money lessons we give our children should go beyond spending, earning, saving, investing, and budgeting. It should include teaching them about generosity and the value of helping others who need financial assistance.

It is difficult to teach children to be financially responsible because they will spend a significant portion of their adult lives earning money and attempting to manage it. As a result, generosity is easily overlooked. Generosity tends to reflect the state of a person's heart. Some people have their finances in order but are not generous. For children to build a habit of generosity, they first have to witness it repeatedly. Try and be a role model in this regard, as it's a win-win situation for everyone. Building a habit of generosity involves allowing them to see how people live, letting them know that just because they are comfortable doesn't mean others are equally fortunate, and even if they are not, that doesn't mean there aren't more people who need more than they do.

Teach them that everybody's story is different. Children tend to see the life they have been exposed to as a measure of everyone's way of life unless we intentionally show them otherwise. Encourage them to be generous, and praise them when you see them being generous and kind. Support them. Talk to them about charities or small ways they can give back. Your children may know a family or two who could need your help, so let them be a part of those acts of generosity. Make it part of your family's culture to assist and help others. This will help them greatly.

Synopsis

Having children and bringing them up in the best way possible is not as easy as it may seem from an outsider's perspective. Being a parent is rewarding and exciting, but it is also a revelation. We must be intentional, especially in a time where the internet is flooded with all sorts of information, accurate and incorrect, good and bad.

What we do from the beginning can shape the financial future of a whole person. This is a huge responsibility, and no parent is perfect. We can all make mistakes, that's only natural. However, we need to learn ways to prevent ourselves from risking all the hard work we put into teaching them and be willing to learn ourselves. Never be ashamed to correct a mistake, as it is your children's future that's at stake.

THE BEST TIME TO HAVE MONEY TALKS WITH YOUR CHILDREN

Teaching your children about money in a digital world should be a continuous effort. Children of all ages should be taught about money. The "when" might be different for different people.

A friend who has two children said she scheduled fifteen minutes daily to have a money conversation with her children: "At the beginning, I used to be particular about teaching them before going to bed, that is before I tell them their bedtime story, but I noticed it became kind of a chore for them and it was taking away the fun. I wanted them to be serious about finances, but at the end of the day they are children, and I did not want them to come to detest it. So, I changed my plan, I made sure I stuck to the fifteen minutes daily at least, though. But this time I gave the lesson whenever the opportunity presented itself. Trust me, it did, many times."

You know best what works for you and your children. Take advantage of every opening and educate them. It does not have to be a boring exercise.

Here are some opportunities you can take advantage of:

- *When they ask you a direct question about finance:* This is not the time to act surprised or coy. You should never ignore the question. Answer them as truthfully as you can, using examples and real-life occurrences to explain your point. If you cannot attend to the question at that moment or if you must research it first, tell them you will give them an answer later. Make sure you give them an answer as soon as possible before they lose interest.
- *Watch out for conversation starters when watching TV:* When watching a TV show or a program, and you spot openings or financial conversation starters, don't ignore them. Pick the most relevant or appropriate moments, though, so you aren't a buzzkill by trying to turn every situation into a money talk.
- *When you go shopping:* Taking your children along when you shop, especially for household supplies, is a good way to have money conversations without trying too hard. You can show them why choosing one product over another would make a difference to your finances. This is how they can learn budgeting, as well as learn about cost and value.

- *When they tell you about other families' finances:* Children talk! They tell each other things. Things they hear, things happening at home, or things in somebody else's home. When a child tells you they heard about a neighbor having a particular financial situation, do not shut them down. This is an opening to teach them a financial lesson.

There are several openings in a day that we get as parents to educate our children. Take them! All you need to do is pay attention and you'll be on your way to maximizing those opportunities. Every life experience may be a chance to have a conversation about money. I think you'll be surprised at just how many opportunities you have!

Who Should Teach Your Children About Money?

We have established that parents have the biggest responsibility when it comes to teaching financial literacy.

Putting it simply, the idea that families can adequately teach their children healthy financial habits is only true in some cases. If we are being truthful, it is challenging for any human, adult or not, to pass on knowledge or a skill they have no clue about. Many parents tell me that they don't feel comfortable teaching their children about money, because they themselves are still trying to "figure it out." Or perhaps they grew up not speaking about money and have no clue how to broach the subject.

The question now is: If children are not learning financial skills at home, what does this mean for future generations? If students cannot count on obtaining a financial education at home, can schools offer them the opportunity? I'm not so sure.

Besides parents, teachers also hold some responsibility for a children's financial education because most children spend more hours in school than they spend anywhere else. However, money matters are not in the curriculum for most educational levels, and even where it is, it's just a little bit here and there.

According to a national report on financial literacy published by Champlain College, 27 states received C grades or lower in financial literacy.

You are probably thinking these children learn math and business studies, but it is not enough because most schools are not required to teach finance-related curriculum.[31]

Over the years, the topic of financial education has been infused into many high school subjects through math, statistics, and business studies. But is it enough to just sprinkle a little financial talk here and there in the curriculum? A Federal Reserve survey of 2018 found that almost 40% of American adults wouldn't be able to cover a $400 emergency with cash, savings, or a credit-card charge that they could quickly pay off. The same survey revealed that 27% of respondents would have to sell their property or borrow from somewhere before they could cover the $400, while 12% of them would not be able to source it at all. Furthermore, the survey found that 12% of adults would be unable to pay their current monthly bills if faced with an unexpected $400 expense. The survey also shows that 56% of the American population has less than $10,000 set aside as their retirement savings.[32]

If those statistics, especially the last one, are not a pointer that we need to take financial education seriously as parents, then I do not know what is. Why? Because if an adult is not financially prepared for future expenses, then that adult is going to struggle with debt, which is why most people still work when they should have retired. To prevent generations of financially ill-prepared citizens, schools should be ready to contribute to the children's financial progress, otherwise the financial future of many children looks bleak.

Lastly, the government is also somewhat responsible for the financial literacy of its citizens.

Although there have been some changes, financial education still differs from one state to another. Some states require it in elementary schools, while others recommend it only to high school students.

Next-Gen Personal Finance (NGPF) led a US-wide investigation of more than 11,000 secondary school course indexes and uncovered a worrying fact: Financial instruction is not being taught in schools. As indicated by the investigation, only one out of six secondary school students needed to take a semester of individual budgeting to be able to graduate.[33]

While some schools are doing the bare minimum, there is clearly a long way to go. We cannot viably teach individual accounting in a condensed manner and expect a magic reversal on the poor money management habits so prevalent around the world. Conventional methodologies, for example, fusing the theme into a more extensive financial matters course, do not allow understudies to participate in genuine encounters where they can cultivate genuine mastery of the financial abilities they need to succeed. The government must make changes in the educational sectors of the states.

Instilling financial skills in children is the responsibility of the parents, teachers, and the government. It would serve individuals and the entire nation to teach children what they need to learn as early as possible.

Are You a Role Model?

Children pic up habits from their parents unknowingly. They often do this unconsciously and "mirror" our behavior. What you keep seeing, you eventually become. This works for both the negative and positive habits we exhibit.

Ann's parents have a piggy bank in their living room. They have had it since they got married, before they had Ann. They come back from a day of work and put in loose change daily. Ann grows up and her parents find that even without teaching her she starts putting money into the piggy bank as well. She gets her allowance and a part of it goes into the piggy bank. When her parents decide that she should get her own piggy bank, Ann is delighted. She finds it easy to set money aside because she has been seeing her parents do it.

Your children are watching you and they model your behavior. This begs the question: What type of financial role model are you?

- Are you an impulsive spender? Or are you a planner, deliberately making decisions about your spending?
- Do you pay your bills and keep them in an organized pile? Or do you let them pile up and leave them lying around?
- Do you save up to make a big purchase? Or do you just purchase without saving and charge it to your credit card?

You are a major influence on your children's financial future, and a lot of it depends on your financial skills. Even if you don't have the best financial skills, you can always learn and in doing so, teach. You cannot squander money and expect to bring up prudent children, although of course there are rare occasions. Getting your own financial skills together is half of the battle if you want to bring up financially literate children. It's important to remember that you can't give what you don't have. If we cannot entirely trust our educational system to instill the financial knowledge they need for their future, the burden is on us to do our best.

Two Families, Two Approaches: Lessons in Financial Education

Here are the stories of two families. Let's call them families A and B.

Each family has two children. The parents of both families tried to give their children the best life possible. It was admirable.

Family A: The parents were big on financial education. They researched schools, but they discovered that no curriculum included full coverage of the subject of financial literacy. They even told their children the reason they were fussy about their school was that they needed them to be financially literate. The parents were disappointed. They wanted their children to get ahead financially. So, what did they do? They got different resources for their children to learn about money: apps and books, amongst other things. The father or the mother would pick up one of the books once or twice a week and ask questions according to what the children were scheduled to study, and on they went. As they reached their teenage years, the children were not the financial experts their parents expected them to be. One of them had maxed out their dad's credit card on a shopping spree. The parents could not help but wonder what they had done wrong. They had tried to prepare them… or did they?

Family B: This household, like household A, was determined to give their children the best financial education. They wanted their children to be able to discuss money, be aware of their financial situation, make healthy money choices, and have their finances in order. The parents had both come from households where money talk was taboo, and money was not considered to be the children's business. When they were children, the parents both learned about money from friends, and they made assumptions about their family's financial status which were deeply exaggerated. At the beginning of the couple's marriage, their finances hit rock bottom, despite combining their already considerable earnings. But they had poor money habits and, whilst individually it was manageable, bringing their terrible money habits together, the problems compounded. (This is an excellent example where the basic rule of minus plus minus is plus does not apply. It is just a longer minus!) It took them accepting their financial deficiencies, getting help, and being more intentional on their part to get their affairs in order. Because of their experience, they became strong advocates for educating their children to be financially responsible. Their own parents had not provided them with a theoretical education on finance, which is why they endeavored to be hands-on with their children, and they understood that they could not give what they did not have. When they finally had children, they started doing all they could: teaching them, telling stories, and turning games into teachable moments, trying to answer as many questions as possible while sharing their experiences with them, which the children found fascinating. Children will make a couple of mistakes along the way, but they'll understand that it was part of the process of continuous learning and every mistake can be a life lesson.

From these experiences, we can see that both families were committed to their children's learning, but their approaches were completely different. And the approach is as important as the commitment. Family A would have had a more successful story if they had also found adequate schools and financial resources for their children. Yet, they still managed to have the money conversations with their children, which made a huge difference. However, they needed to go beyond simply asking them questions about books they read about finance. It would have made a big difference.

Family A could have enhanced their financial education approach by actively involving their children in real-life money management scenarios, such as budgeting for weekly expenses or setting savings goals. In contrast, Family B not only had money conversations but also provided practical experiences like involving their children in family financial discussions and decision-making, allowing them to develop a deeper understanding of money management from a young age.

Please, have the money conversations with your children. It might not be the easiest task, but it benefits both parties. Be responsible for a huge fraction of your children's financial education. Do not leave it to chance. *Never* leave it to chance.

HAVING THE CONVERSATION: WHY TALKING ABOUT MONEY MATTERS

Have a plan and have a budget.

– Emmanuel Asuquo

It's important to have conversations about spending, saving, and budgeting while engaging in everyday activities together.

For example, weave in some of these conversations after dinner. Choose a topic. It can be even the simplest things, like identifying the head and tail sides of a coin or differentiating different bills. Making this a regular occurrence gets children more comfortable about discussing money.

Many parents spend most of their time trying to get children to retain the things they have taught them and may get frustrated if their child forgets or slips up. While this is great, the main purpose is to first accelerate the frequency of money discussions, rather than quizzing them on what they remember.

Let your conversations be age-appropriate. An 8-year-old is likely to understand more things than a 5-year-old. Discuss coins and other simple concepts with younger children, and you can go further with older children by discussing the benefits of earning an allowance.

Such a conversation can take place anywhere, like at a bank or the ATM. Banking has become dynamic over the years (for instance, you don't need to visit banks anymore for 95% of transactions), but it is still a good idea to take your children to see a bank or ATM for themselves so they can understand what it is and what it does. Remember, the goal is to give them an experience.

Let Them Spend Their Money

Children often want a lot of things, especially with the influence of television and social media. Even if you have the means to buy them whatever they want, it's crucial to still let them spend their own money. Children even get *more* excited and feel prouder of their new toy when they pay for it themselves. You would be surprised. As I have said several times so far, you must let your children practice all the things you teach them. Allow them the opportunity to make mistakes. They will learn from them when the stakes are low.

If you don't want to spend real money right away, play money is also great for this. (You can also make it yourself.) We do this often with my daughter's toy kitchen and a game called "eat out." As guests, of course, we had to pay for the food and she gave me change. (The first time, however, she asked us for a credit card.)

RECAP

Teaching children about money from an early age is essential for their financial literacy and future success. In this guide, I provide you with practical tips to introduce financial concepts in age-appropriate ways, ensuring your children develop a healthy relationship with money.

Start with basic concepts like understanding money, saving, and role modeling good financial habits. Include your children in everyday financial activities, such as managing bank accounts, charitable giving, and setting financial goals. Emphasize the importance of planning, saving, and patience. Use your children's questions as teachable moments to explain credit, debt, and financial priorities.

Incorporate financial education into play using games and practical experiences like shopping. Teach generosity by encouraging charitable acts and empathy. Lead by example with good financial habits and maintain open discussions about money. Avoid common mistakes like leaving children to learn on their own, avoiding the topic, or over-controlling their spending.

Advocate for comprehensive financial literacy programs in schools and provide additional resources to enhance your children's learning.

By making financial discussions a regular part of family life and involving your children in practical financial activities, you can help ensure they grow up to be financially literate and responsible. Remember, it's never too young to start teaching your children about money.

EARNING 2

One day, my 6-year-old daughter was holding a Swiss ten-Franc bill and her stuffed toy (a duck she calls Paperetti), who she adored. I playfully suggested to her that I ease her burden by holding her ten-Franc bill for her. She audaciously responded in a tone I found very amusing, "Money is not a burden." Her comment made me laugh hard because it was amazing to see how much she had already learned. Others would argue that she is her father's daughter—the child of someone who has worked in banks for decades. However, it wasn't just that. Children become aware of money as a concept at an early age. They might not know all the intricate details about it, but they are aware that it has some sort of value. At that stage, when they are in preschool or elementary school, they are curious about everything. They know that money is important, and it is your duty as a parent to let them know in the simplest ways possible *how* important money is and all the things they can do with it.

Have your children ever asked you to buy them toys or candy, and you told them you did not have the money on hand? Have you received an aghast look and a response that says, "You *don't* have money?" These kinds of questions and surprised responses underscore how children start to connect the concept of money with the ability to obtain goods, illustrating the beginning of their journey in financial literacy.

I am not sure if it is the fact that they do not see cash often, but they are very curious about money, especially cash. Maybe it is because of its haptic properties (relating to the sense of touch). Work on piquing their curiosity instead of suppressing it. They might be too young to understand all the complex details about money, but you can still work around their curiosity and teach them in tiny steps. What we teach children at this point has a significant impact on their lives. They are so impressionable when they are young, so we must impress upon them the right things. They might not have the range to learn all the complex details at that time in their life, but you can still set them on the right path.

We have established the fact that children, even aged 5 to 8, are aware of money and the value it possesses. They can fully differentiate between bills and coins. A good place to start is to try and find out how much they know, because children at this age tend to be more open to sharing information. Teach them about different bills and help them identify them. They need to know that each unit of money has its value.

Bills available for use today include the $1, $2, $5, $10, $20, $50, and $100 notes.

The main idea is to convey the concept of a financial unit, which is to say the value of one dollar. Coins are only parts of that unit; bills are products of that unit. 100 cents equals one dollar, etc.

Understanding that cash depends on the dollar unit allows you to talk about the concept of reciprocals: that 10 pennies are equivalent to one dime in the United States; that 10 dimes are equivalent to one green dollar.

Make this learning process as fun as possible. You can teach them simple things like heads and tails and how to identify both sides. You can tell them where the money comes from, in simple terms, which can be the beginning of a wonderful and ongoing conversation about the value of hard work.

The important thing your child needs to know is the fact that money is based on the dollar, that coins are just one piece of that unit, and that different bills are simply many dollar units. This allows you to further explain that 10 pennies are equivalent to 1 dime, while 4 quarters is equivalent to 1 dollar bill. You can ask them how many coins it takes to make 50 cents, then you can repeat the same process for larger amounts.

MONEY AS A TOOL FOR EXCHANGE

My curious 6-year-old daughter asked me why she could not pay for candy with paper because money was also paper. I thought this was a valid question, because, why not? Children ask questions like this all the time. Never laugh them off. Give an intelligent but simple answer. One of the best and easiest ways to explain the perceived value of money to children is by explaining the barter system to them.

Here is How I Would Approach the Question

"A long time ago, people did not have everything they needed, so they needed to buy goods like we do now. The difference was that they did not have money. So, let's say great-grandpa William wanted soap and he had a jar of jam, which was of the same value, or almost the same value, as the soap. He would look for someone who had soap and was willing to accept jam in exchange. This was called barter. It was a simple process, which involved exchanging one thing for another without using money. This process worked for them for a while because they did not have another option. But after a while, it became difficult because you might want to exchange your shoes for a dress but nobody wanted a pair of shoes. People did not always want what you had to exchange. So, it became imperative for them to have a generally acceptable item for exchange. This was where money came in. Instead of exchanging your soap for a jar of jam, you could get soap with money. It is still a form of exchange but now with a generally accepted currency."

Explain the barter system with items that they can relate to. Use everyday household items to depict how the barter system has been replaced with money.

TEACHING CHILDREN ABOUT EARNING AND THE ATM

> *40% of 5-year-olds think money from the ATM is free.*
> *– Commonwealth Bank of Australia*

ATM Stories

The following ATM stories are real stories from casual conversations I had with other parents as I researched this topic. (Yes, I talk about financial literacy on the playground. But only when people ask me what I do!) I came across, as you would expect, hilarious stories of children and their experiences with ATMs, or their expectations of the machines. Here are a few:

- "After I told him I did not have money to buy him a new toy, Thomas, my 7-year-old, got dressed to go to the ATM to get money to buy his toy himself."
- "I took my 6-year-old daughter to use the ATM and she couldn't believe her eyes. I noticed that she was quiet on

our way back home. We got home and she asked me, 'Mom, are you going to go to the ATM again to get money?' I said, 'Yes, when I need it.' She then said thoughtfully, 'Why didn't you just take all the money we will need forever so you do not have to go back to the ATM?' I laughed my heart out."

- "Michael thinks that I own the ATM and I have an unlimited supply of money. He asked me once why we couldn't bring the ATM to our house instead of going all the way to make a withdrawal. I knew I had work to do at that point."

- "I was teaching my children about earning money and how I went to work every morning to earn money for the family. I explained how the money that we spend comes from what I am paid. I was painting a picture of the work dynamics when my daughter raised curious eyes to me and said simply: 'You do not have to work, though.' When I asked why, she said, 'Because we have the ATM, and we can go and get money for the family anytime we want.'"

- "My son came home to tell me that his friend was changing schools because 'his parents did not have money anymore' (his words). But he told me he'd found a solution, and he did not know why they did not think of it in the first place. He seemed so proud. I just had to hear the solution my little 5-year-old proffered. He said he told them to 'go to the ATM and they could get all the money they need.' That wasn't the part that almost made me choke with laugher. He said his friend had told him that his parents used the ATM too, but they still did not have money anymore. My son suggested to his friend that he tell his parents to use the ATM we use because money never ends in that one. I was howling with laughter by the time he finished."

- "I had been taking my children to use the ATM for a few months. One day, we were done and as were leaving my children called my attention to a man who was using the ATM after we did, and said, 'He is trying to take our money, dad.' I had to give him a long-overdue lecture on the workings of the ATM."
- "My son came home and asked me if we were poor. I was shocked because we were nothing close to poor, and I'd assumed he knew that. He told me his classmate said his dad had a machine that gave them money. Only rich people used the machine. This was in elementary school. I did not hesitate; I took my son to the ATM and gave him a lesson. It got me thinking about how, when we fail to teach our children certain things, they may end up learning them from the wrong source. I know that he would have eventually figured out that what his classmate was saying wasn't the truth, but a little damage may have been done before that happened."
- "My husband took our children to use the ATM and our daughter was fascinated by the fact that money was coming out of the machine. Her sitter took her out for a walk one day and she said she wanted to stop at the ATM to get money. Her sitter asked why she thought she could do that, and she responded that with Mom and Dad she did it all the time."
- "I took my daughter to use the ATM for the first time, and she looked at me accusingly when she saw money coming out of the machine. I asked what the look was for and she said, 'You told me you work for money.'"

Debunking ATM Myths

ATM stories are amusing, but the hard truth is that children sometimes assume that money just shows up. We must teach them that money is earned.

For example, you could take the opportunity to explain that you go to work daily and, because of the work you do, you get paid at the end of every month. Or, if you are an entrepreneur, you can explain to them that the people pay you for the products or services you offer and that is where the money to provide for the family comes from. Then, the money you earn is put in a bank that is connected to your debit card, which is what you take out every time you use the ATM.

You can use a piggybank as an example. When they put money in the piggy bank it stays there until they are ready to take it out. Or you could have a token piggy bank with some coins and notes and a token credit card to mimic the scenario of taking money out and show that when the money runs out there's nothing to take out. They cannot remove from their piggy bank what they did not put inside it. Similarly, the money you withdraw from the ATM is money you have put in the bank.

The piggy bank illustration always does the trick. For instance, my bank account is my *electronic piggy bank* from which I can withdraw money. The ATM is like the opening slot. With this explanation, the underlying principle was understood directly and WITHOUT any additional questions from my daughter.

Teaching Children to Manage Their First Earnings

Children eagerly await the arrival of the tooth fairy or their birthday. The tooth fairy is known for leaving money and most children receive at least some money for their birthdays.

It is your responsibility to prepare them to responsibly receive money. Show them the many things they can do with money: They can choose to spend, save, invest, or share it. Give them lessons that encourage them to spend money wisely because it will run out. At this early age they need your guidance, and, as hard as it might be, give them a little leeway. Let them decide what they want to do, to a certain degree. If they make a mistake, they will learn a valuable lesson (usually that money spent is gone) and they will most likely be wiser next time.

I was upset a couple of years ago when I saw one of my friends give his son a $100 bill. The teenager took the bill and turned away to leave as if nothing just happened. He did not say anything, not even a *thank you* or a smile. He just kept a straight face and turned to leave. I could see the disappointment in his father's face as he asked: "Won't you say anything? Not even thank you?" I know my face turned red when I heard the child respond: "This allowance is nothing compared to what my friends get from their parents. Besides, it is my money. But, thank you, I need it anyway." (To be honest, I would have taken the money back from him right away.)

The 14-year-old put the money in his pocket and walked away like he was the winner of a competition, while I stared at his father's sorrowful expression.

This is a typical example of the toxic entitlement mentality common among children these days. I have seen this happen in many different ways. Parents have become ATMs for their children.

Money is particularly important, and it carries great lessons. The way you handle it, the way you relate with another person using money, determines the message you will put across to that person. Yes, you have been passing a money message on to your children all the while you have been giving them allowances.

> *If you want your children to have an unfair advantage in life, teach them financial education. Show them the real rules of money and taxes.*
>
> – Robert T. Kiyosaki

Robert T. Kiyosaki, author of *Rich Dad Poor Dad*, told the story of how his rich dad taught him a vital lesson of how money can control people and you can convey messages and lessons through money.

A Short Story From Rich Dad Poor Dad

When Robert Kiyosaki was a kid, he went to the same school as the rich kids, even though he didn't live on the same side of town. Because of his financial situation, he sought a solution to the question "How can I make money?"

Robert's best friend, Mike, was similarly disadvantaged. On a Saturday morning, the two of them discussed ways to make money. One of these ways was an unlawful one: forging nickels out of lead. The two went back to the drawing board after Robert Kiyosaki's father explained to them the penalties of counterfeiting.

Robert's father (Poor Dad) suggested that the two learn money-making skills from his wealthy grandfather (Rich Dad). His banker had informed him about his rich father's ability to accumulate money. Rich Dad scheduled a meeting with the two, and they began learning together.

Robert Kiyosaki went to Rich Dad at 8:00 a.m., on schedule and prepared for the meeting. Rich Dad assured the two boys that he would be delighted to teach them, but not in the typical school environment. He suggested that the two boys work for him so that he could train them. They didn't have a choice on how to proceed as they didn't want to miss the opportunity. Opportunities come and go, so grasping them while they are still available is vital. Rich Dad offered to pay Robert and Mike ten cents an hour for three hours on Saturdays every week.

After a few weeks of painstaking work, Robert told Mike that he was quitting. This is exactly the reaction Rich Dad had hoped for.

Poor Dad told him to demand a raise, at least 25 cents an hour, and to quit if he didn't get the raise, before meeting with Rich Dad. Robert was upset because he had to wait an hour longer than usual to meet Rich Dad. Robert felt Rich Dad had broken his side of the bargain by making Robert work tirelessly for him and was simply taking advantage of him.

After a month, Robert began to sound like one of Rich Dad's employees. Rich Dad, however, argued that he was teaching Robert in a non-schooling manner. That, compared to reading books, action was the most efficient method of learning.

On that day, Robert was advised by Rich Dad that he could either become like his workers, who blamed others for their problems, or he might choose a different path and become a very wealthy person.

Instead of working for someone else, Rich Dad suggested that the two kids find a new way to make money by simply working for themselves even if they were still working for someone else. He explained that the only way to be rich and wealthy was to work for yourself, however, they needed to start by working for someone else.

The question is whether money manages you or you manage money.

MONEY, SURVIVAL, AND THE PRINCIPLE OF EXCHANGE

Before Money

Think of how society was before money existed. Human beings lived for tens of thousands of years as hunters and gatherers, existing off the land without a formal currency system. As we stopped our nomadic ways and settled in the first cities, the barter system naturally developed, with different farmers specializing in different crops or arts. Then, as civilization grew and expanded, the barter system became too weak. Economic activities and exchange habits became more complex than the barter system could handle, so there was a need for money. For instance, imagine a scenario where a farmer who specialized in growing wheat wanted to acquire a pair of shoes. In the barter system, the farmer would have to find a shoemaker who needed wheat and was willing to exchange shoes for it. However, if the shoemaker didn't need wheat or didn't want to trade shoes at that particular time, the farmer would have to find another person who wanted wheat and had something the shoemaker desired. This process of finding a suitable trading partner and negotiating mutually beneficial exchanges became increasingly challenging and time-consuming as economic activities expanded, leading to the need for a more efficient medium of exchange, which is money.

Back then, power resided in the hands of those who had something valuable to exchange. For example, if you had a yam barn, then you were all set because you could easily exchange your yams for any other thing you needed.

After Money

Things changed after money entered our society and replaced the simple trading of goods and services. Now, it's an integral part of our existence, history, and culture. You cannot, for instance, pay your school fees by giving the school management sacks of yams or cups of rice. You need money to exchange goods and services essential for your survival. It is hard to survive and go through life without it.

Robert Kiyosaki puts it like this: Because money is linked with personal survival, if you have money, you can get people to do things they may not necessarily want to do. Things such as getting up and going to work every day or studying hard so you can get a good job.

The association of money with personal survival gives it immense power, enabling individuals to manipulate and influence others' behaviors and actions in pursuit of their own interests and goals.

Principle of Exchange

The principle of exchange is one of the most important money concepts you should teach your children. Real life is all about exchange. You can't get anything out of life if you do not have something of value to exchange for it. The principle is quite simple; the more you give, the more you get.

This applies in all areas of life. Many parents are poor today because they were not taught that life and money are all about exchange. The bigger the value you exchange, the bigger the value you get back. Hence, a driver might work from morning to night on the road and not make half the money a real estate investor or agent will get by closing a deal in 20 minutes. The difference? It is not in the length of hours put in, it is in the value being exchanged or put more simply, the value of goods being sold. A real estate agent is offering a home, the driver is offering a specific service for a specific price. One is more valuable, of course.

The Magic of Mutual Benefit

Now you see how important it is that children start learning and understanding the principle of exchange. This is the very first thing I teach people whenever they ask me about financial intelligence or literacy.

This is, for instance, the reason I never offer a free service*, no matter who is asking because, if I do, I would be breaking a particularly important financial rule that the person might never

---

* I work as "Der Textcoach" (www.textcoa.ch) and solve writing problems of my clients.

learn again. There must be something to exchange for the value you get.

After a conference, a young man walked up to me. With tears in his eyes, he told me how he was in a bad situation and he did not have a dime to his name. He asked if I could help him. I understood his situation, as it was not the first time I had met someone like that. When he finished his request, I asked the all-important question: "How much would you pay me to teach you everything?" The looks on the faces of those who heard me ask the question said, *Seriously?*

The man thought I had not heard everything he had said countless times before. He was about to start the narration from the beginning, but I did not let him. I had heard him the first time, and I meant the question I asked. Do you think it was mean and uncompassionate? Well, asking for something in exchange for anything was the first lesson I was teaching him, but he wanted pity instead.

Synopsis

We should teach children to understand that they must provide value to get value in return, and the bigger their value, the bigger what they get in return. They should never expect anything for free, so they should always be ready and prepared to give to receive.

The Value of Money and Allowance (Pocket Money)

Allowances can be extremely beneficial for children to learn about money, but you must go about it the right way. For example, there is no "end all be all" recommendation for allowances as every child, home, and family financial situation differs. Various factors should influence how much allowance you give your children, how you pay them, etc.

In my experience, it's best to give children monthly allowances and teenagers weekly allowances. Be careful not to give them allowances that would allow them to spend frivolously. Just ensure the amount of money you give them will cover basic primary expenses and then take care of some fun expenses. This means you will need to consider the cost of things and your children's ability to manage and use money wisely. You should consider whether your child has a part-time job or not before you give them an allowance, which will also depend on how old they are.

Basically, the allowance should cover all expenses you expect your children to take care of (e.g., hobbies, personal items, gifts, and entertainment) and discretionary (or fun) spending, as well as some left over to be able to save or invest. All allowances should be in cash. Do not rush to bail them out when they run out of money or spend all of their allowance before the next one comes.

(See the next chapter below for more on allowances.)

Money Lessons Through Part-Time Work

The principle of exchange is not the only important money principle you should teach your children. It is only the foundation for other important things your children should learn. There are a couple of other lessons behind the principle of exchange. Even though money is a powerful teaching tool, there are far more important lessons for your children to learn that underline everything else. It is the lessons behind the lessons that are most important. And one of those is the lesson on the importance of working (or offering their services in exchange for money).

To make money, you must either provide a service (work/jobs) or sell items. This might inspire them to look for part-time work. Children can lawfully work part-time beginning at the age of 14.[34] This includes, for instance, light work during school holidays where the hours do not exceed 7 in any day or 35 in any week.[35] (Disclaimer: Please note that I am not a U.S. attorney. Due to the changing nature of laws, please always check the applicable rules with the authorities of your jurisdiction.)

Before you allow your child to apply for a part-time job, ensure that there would be a good balance between homework, social activities, and other important things. Getting a part-time job is important; it will do more than put more money in your child's pocket. A part-time job exposes your children to work experiences that are bound to be useful in the future. For instance, a part-time job could give them a clue as to what they want to do or study in the future.

My friend Christopher is doing great right now as a chef. And, guess what? He did not have any clue about food until he decided to work for Lufthansa's Sky Chefs in a part-time job at the age of seventeen. It was while he was working there that he developed an interest in food. He became crazy about it and pursued a career as a chef.

Your child can also learn some basic life and financial skills while working a part-time job. Things like handling communication, pressure, interpersonal conflict, and time management, as well as multitasking and dressing professionally are all important skills for teenagers to learn.

Part-time jobs can also build your child's self-esteem and confidence. If they do well and make some money, they will likely believe in themselves more. Self-esteem and confidence are vital in building wealth and succeeding in professional careers or studies. They will need that now and in the future. There are loads of benefits in taking part-time jobs aside from just making money. Show your children how important all of it is and teach them why they should take on part-time jobs. When discussing the importance of part-time jobs with your children, consider emphasizing the practical skills they can gain, such as time management, responsibility, and teamwork. Encourage them to explore different job opportunities that align with their interests and passions, as this can enhance their overall learning experience. Additionally, highlight the value of saving and budgeting their earnings to instill financial responsibility and long-term planning habits.

While you support your children to take on part-time jobs, you also must be careful. All the advantages of taking part-time jobs should be measured against how they would cope with school and other commitments if they start a part-time job. You must understand that all children are different, and they have different capacities and abilities. While some will be able to manage their education, a job, and other parts of their life comfortably, it might be a huge struggle for other children.

If your children fall into the latter category, then they should consider doing summer part-time jobs when they don't have to worry about schoolwork.

IMPORTANT EARNING AND INVESTMENT LESSONS

Jobs Will Not Make Them Rich

Now is the time to strengthen and teach your children an important lesson: Jobs will not make them rich. So many young people spend all their lives studying and acquiring skills to look for jobs, and they have high hopes that they will get high-paying jobs when they graduate from college or their training. This is generally not the case.

At this stage, you will see them freelancing and juggling different jobs. Working longer and harder is great, but it will not make them rich in the real world. Making good financial decisions will make one wealthy.

The reason for this is quite simple: You have limited time, limited energy, and even limited jobs, so jumping from jobs or simply working more does have a limit. Look at it this way: If you are paid $50 per hour and work for five hours in a day, at the end of the day, you will have made $250. Let's say you want to improve your earnings, so what will you do about it? You might decide to increase the number of hours you work, so you may start working seven hours per day. As a result, you will start earning $350 per day, but that will come with additional stress. There is a limit to how long you can work during the day. Even if you want to stretch yourself to the limit, you cannot exceed 24 hours per day.

If you still want to earn more, you will not be able to increase the number of hours, so you will probably look for another job that pays more. High-paying jobs are scarce and often take much of your time and energy due to the level of responsibility and demand for exceptional performance and results. But it's not just limited to this. It is often the case that public exposure in these positions is greater, so you must be available to stakeholders outside normal working hours as well. Additionally, a high-paying job of course means higher taxes. People keep running the loop of looking for a job, getting paid, quitting their jobs for better ones, and then quitting again, until they retire poor.

Your children should be aware of this before they make decisions based on the notion that working is the answer to accumulating wealth. Over the years, they might have seen investments as just another way to make extra income, but they must start seeing investments as a structured and established way to get rich. If your children want to be rich, they need to change their mindset about money and how it flows. They need to stop thinking about who to work for and how many jobs they can do to become wealthy because, again, jobs never make people wealthy. A job might set them off on that journey, but being wealthy means building sustainable wealth and having financial freedom such that you do not have to work actively to make money or survive.

So, what should we do then?

Investments and Compound Interest

Teach your children how to work and save smarter through the power of investing. When age-appropriate, teaching about compound interest will far better prepare them for the real world than only preaching about work. One potential route to wealth can be through investments and the power of compound interest.

I currently work as a freelance writer. I write and create material for books and businesses, and I am compensated for each of them. Some pay handsomely, while others pay little, but that isn't the point. Some of my clients have published their books on Amazon Kindle and other online bookstores. Some clients additionally print and sell thousands of hard copies of their book. Now consider this: I was paid, and they sold their books for a good price, but there is a significant difference. They are still in business, selling their books on various platforms all over the world, whilst I was only paid once for the work I did.

Let's say I wrote a book and was paid $1,000. Then the author publishes it on, say, Amazon for $50 per copy. He only needs 200 people to buy the book to recover the money he paid me for developing the content. Then, after that, he keeps selling the book. Say the book becomes a best seller and hundreds and thousands of people buy it all over the world. He might end up making millions of dollars for a book he paid someone $1,000 to write. Plus, there's no limit on how long the book can be sold. Now, the authors I wrote for are investors serving an unlimited number of people while I am just a freelance writer myself and earning little.

If some people knew this earlier in their life, they would certainly have accumulated more assets. Therefore, it is essential to initiate discussions about investments and wealth-building with children when they reach their teenage years. Approach the conversation by first instilling the value of saving money and setting financial goals. As they grasp these concepts, introduce the idea of investing and its potential for growth over time. Regarding teaching what you may not know yourself, you can first explore external resources like books, online courses, and experts. Encourage continuous learning and financial literacy to equip them with the necessary knowledge and skills.

The truth is, there are some things they need to learn now that you might not be able to teach them yourself if you are not investment savvy.

This does not mean they should not take on jobs. You will get to know examples of part-time jobs in the next chapter. They should look for jobs as previously described, but only as a route to investing more and engaging the power of compound interest. This should also encourage them to take savings seriously. The worst thing to do is to spend all their money from their part-time job and "live from salary to salary." You can keep giving them allowances until they are out of college and get their first full-time job with a consistent pay.

Just let me briefly explain why investments and compound interest are such important concepts. Please look at the graph below, which shows the effect of compound interest and how money grows over time. The same can be applied to almost any type of investment. In my example, I used a principal amount of $1,000, an annual interest rate of 5%, compounded monthly over 20 years.

EARNING

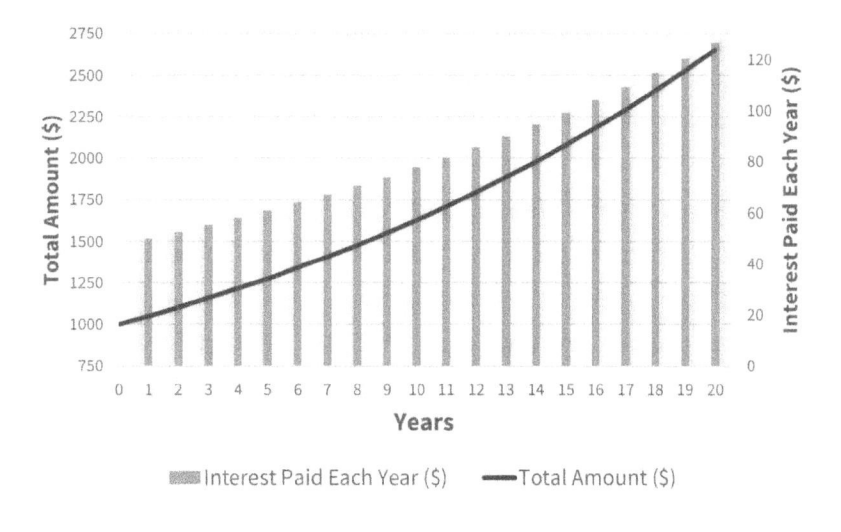

Compound Interest Growth over time

When you look at the graph, you can easily recognize that compound interest is so amazing because it turbocharges your savings by letting you earn interest on your initial investment and the interest accumulates over time. This snowball effect accelerates your wealth growth, making it a financial powerhouse!

Earning vs. Life Balance

Teach your children how to handle money and not allow your job to affect other parts of your life. Many children will grow up and find it difficult to manage their lives while working or chasing money. They will keep finding out that life is manic and difficult to manage. For instance, your child may struggle to balance school responsibilities, extracurricular activities, and part-time jobs. Children might find themselves overwhelmed with commitments and unable to find enough time for rest, relaxation, or their interests. Additionally, children may experience stress and anxiety from juggling multiple responsibilities, leading to difficulties in managing their emotions and overall well-being. This example highlights the tangible impact of life's manic and difficult nature on a child's ability to navigate their daily life effectively. There is a pervasive failure in society to find balance between building a career, maintaining a family, and developing other parts of their life. A lot of parents do not spend time at home because they are working somewhere far from home or have a busy schedule to help them pay the bills. Money costs family time, amongst many other things. Or, to put it in other words: The pursuit of money can have a negative impact on the amount of time you can spend with you child and the overall quality of family relationships. When you are consistently occupied with work or take on additional jobs to make ends meet, it leaves you with less availability and energy to dedicate to your family.

As a result, overworking limits the opportunities for bonding, communication, and shared experiences between you and your child. Your child will then probably feel a sense of emotional distance or neglect, as your absence or preoccupation with work becomes a regular part of their life. The lack of quality time and parental involvement may have consequences on your child's emotional well-being, self-esteem, and overall development. Furthermore, when money becomes the primary focus, other important aspects of life such as family values, personal well-being, and nurturing relationships may take a back seat. Your child may observe that financial success comes at the expense of other essential aspects of life, leading to an imbalance and potential dissatisfaction in the long run.

By highlighting the cost of money on family time, you can emphasize the importance of finding a balance between financial stability and maintaining meaningful connections within your family.

You must teach your children to learn how to manage money alongside other parts of their lives. One of the first things to do is to show them that lots of jobs and hard work will not make them rich. If they learn this, they will be able to start building wealth. And in the future, when they have their own family, they will not find themselves in a situation where they must give up things for a job. Money will be working for them while they take care of their body, family, faith, etc.

EARNING FOR PRETEENS (AGES 9 TO 12)

While the legal work age doesn't start until the teens, your child can begin trading services for money starting around age 9. Starting jobs early not only teaches about money, but also responsibility. Children are usually eager to start earning because it gives them an additional income, separate from their allowance. The job types and compensation for such odd jobs will depend on location. The difficulty and the length of time to complete each job will also vary. Here are a few job options for your children at that age.

It's important to ensure that a job does not replace an allowance but rather complements it. Allowances provide a steady base for financial learning, while jobs offer a practical application of earning money. Parents should avoid lowering the allowance when their child starts a job, as the two sources of income serve different educational purposes.

Babysitting

Your preteen can earn money by babysitting younger children for neighbors, extended family, or friends. There are babysitting trainings and certifications for children. The Red Cross offers one of those training opportunities for preteens age 11 and above called "Babysitting Basics-online."[36] The natures of the jobs may differ. There are also babysitting opportunities where the mother stays home with the babysitter and the babysitter acts more like a helper to the mother. This is a great option to consider if you don't think your child is ready to stay home alone.

Manning a Lemonade Stand (or Yard Sale)

This is usually the number one idea most parents have when thinking of accessible business ideas for their children's financial improvement. The business is no doubt good for your children's financial education and character building. It also teaches them the value of return on their effort if they're the ones making the lemonade too.

Lawn Mowing or Shoveling Snow

There is always that neighbor who is too busy to mow their lawn or who just hates to mow it. This would be a good job to consider for your children if they like being outdoors and if they don't mind manual labor. These jobs may be continuous or occasional when the homeowner is not available. Your children can use your mower or their employer's.

Yardwork

There are many other outdoor tasks that a homeowner may need help with besides mowing their lawns. These can be tasks such as raking leaves, helping with planting in the garden, snow shoveling, etc. Your child can do any of these jobs during their spare time and holidays. They can do them alone or with the homeowner.

Dog Walking

This would be a good job for kids who love pets. It is also a good way to get your child to exercise, and who doesn't like killing two birds with one stone? You should make sure your child, the pet, and the pet's parents are all comfortable with one another before walking or pet sitting.

Delivering Papers

Many children, especially early risers, consider this fun (again, it was for me!). You might have to regulate this, decide with them what to do on a rainy day, and decide how comfortable you are sending your 9-year-old out alone in the early hours of the morning around the neighborhood. Work out their schedule. They can make weekly deliveries if daily deliveries would affect any of their other activities.

Family Business

Do you have a business or a workplace where you child could work? For example, if you have an office, your child could help with filing papers, mailing letters, and other minor office work. You can also work around their school schedule. This is a great weekend job for children and a good bonding experience for the family.

Modern Earning Opportunities for Kids and Teens

In today's digital age, there are numerous ways for children and teenagers to earn money beyond traditional part-time jobs. Digital platforms and social media offer innovative opportunities that cater to their interests and skills.

Many young people are turning to platforms like YouTube, TikTok, and Instagram to create content and share their passions. (But please always keep in mind the risks that these platforms pose!) Whether your children are making videos about their hobbies, creating tutorials, or simply vlogging about their daily lives, these platforms allow them to monetize their content through ads, sponsorships, and viewer donations. It's important to guide them on ways to maintain privacy and safety while online.

Websites like Fiverr and Upwork offer opportunities for teens to freelance in various fields such as graphic design, writing, video editing, and programming. These platforms allow them to gain real-world experience, build their portfolio, and earn money by working on projects that interest them.

Platforms like Etsy enable creative kids and teens to sell handmade crafts, artwork, and other products. This not only allows them to make money but also teaches them about running a business, marketing, and customer service.

Websites like Swagbucks and Survey Junkie pay users to participate in surveys and market research. While the earnings might not be substantial, it's a simple way for teens to make some extra money in their spare time.

For those who enjoy video games, platforms like Twitch and YouTube Gaming offer the chance to earn money by streaming their gameplay. They can receive donations, subscriptions, and sponsorships from viewers who enjoy watching their content.

These modern earning opportunities not only provide financial benefits but also teach valuable skills such as digital literacy, entrepreneurship, and time management. Encouraging children and teenagers to explore these options can help them develop a strong work ethic and an understanding of how to leverage their talents in the digital world.

Whatever your children decide to do, guide them and assist them as much as you can. The benefits of them getting a job are innumerable. Mostly, it makes them financially responsible, and this is a vital part of their financial education.

THINGS TO CONSIDER WHEN MAKING EARNING DECISIONS FOR TEENAGERS (AGES 13 TO 17)

Should Your Child Get a Job?

I have met some parents that think their children should not be doing part-time jobs for personal reasons.

Some parents do not want their teenager to be working while in school. Some claim they don't need the cash. Others say they don't want their teenager to focus on a short-term job and lose sight of their long-term goals. However, there are many benefits to kids working part-time, beyond them getting an income.

Alternatives to Part-Time Jobs

If you prefer for your child not to take up a job, you could encourage them to join a volunteer group instead. These volunteer groups provide the right conditions and opportunities to experience and learn some of the things I already mentioned, but they may be less demanding in terms of time commitment. Volunteer positions are often available in hospitals, museums, and other organizations.

Importance of Early Work Experiences

Consider your child's early work experiences (or volunteer positions) as particularly important. They are some of the several big firsts in their life and you should be there to support them and cheer them on just like you did when they took their first steps. If they fall, lift them up and encourage them. If they keep walking, motivate them on and celebrate with them. Imagine your child facing a setback at their first part-time job. Let's say your child lands a part-time job at a local store and struggles with certain tasks or makes mistakes that affect their confidence. As a supportive parent, you can lift your child up by providing words of encouragement, reminding them that mistakes are part of the learning process, and offering guidance on how to improve. By showing understanding and empathy, you can help your child regain confidence and motivation to keep going. If your child overcomes these initial challenges and shows progress, celebrate the achievements, no matter how small. This boosts your child's self-esteem and reinforces determination to excel in their job.

This is important to them, too. Whatever path they choose, whatever part-time job they decide to do, let the attention and focus be on learning all that they can in addition to making money.

The very first time they do things like write a resume, fill out a job application, or prepare for interviews, celebrate them and make these a great lesson for them. Make sure you help them go through it. They are experiences they will need in the future.

Considerations Before Your Child Gets a Job

Like I mentioned before, many parents are not always sure if their children should start working or if they are ready to get a job. I have put together some basic factors you should look at when making that decision.

1. *Reliability:* How reliable is your child? Can you trust him or her to be punctual and take on responsibilities? Keep an eye on this. From the way they handle responsibilities and carry out tasks at home, you can tell if they can handle responsibilities in the workplace. If they are not that reliable, then you can help them improve this at home before getting a job, although sometimes getting a job is the way for them to learn. They might have a negative experience like getting the sack later or hating the job, but that is education. This is where you also check how well they can handle balancing the responsibilities of schoolwork, home, life, and friends.

2. *Maturity:* This is the second factor to consider. The work environment and demands from a job are quite different from those at home. At home, there are rarely any deadlines and pressure, where at work, one might face an angry boss or even punishment if they slip up. It takes a mature mind to act professionally. Mistakes at home at worst will get them grounded, but mistakes at work will get them sacked.

Your child should be able to manage different relationships with colleagues and supervisors. It takes maturity to switch between these different roles effectively.

The questions here are:

- Are they mature enough to handle themselves professionally in a job situation?
- Can they take the demands of a job seriously?
- Can they make the sacrifice of spending less time with their friends to have time for a job?

Another particularly important question to consider here is whether they are confident and bold enough to express themselves in the workplace if they have problems or concerns regarding the job. You do not want a situation where your child keeps quiet when they are being taken advantage of in the workplace or instances where they can't negotiate properly.

3. *Independence:* This is all about children developing the right mindset and deciding to be effective and productive. You will not be around all the time, and you should not have to push them to do everything. You must check how self-reliant they are. Will they sleep all day if you do not wake them up for school? Do they do chores and assignments at home without a reminder? How often do they use their intuition to know what ought to be done at home? Can they manage their own time effectively without anything having to give? Can they go to work on their own and come back on their own? Make sure you consider and ask all these questions and more to test how effective and efficient they can be on their own.

4. *Motivation:* Motivation is key to success. The reason for considering all these is to make sure your children have the right mindset before they leave your home. To prepare them to be successful and to survive outside of the confines of home and school. First, does your child want a job? If they don't, there is a chance that things will go wrong so it is better they don't start working at the moment. If they think they are not ready and do not want a job just yet, then let them be for a while and try to help them see the value of a job, so they may change their mind about it. Talk to them about other options like volunteering.

Do not make up for their financial lag when they begin to run low on money, but do not ignore them either. Talk to them about ways they can earn money or just ask them what plans they have to increase their earnings. There are lots of options through which they can make money.

Some children are simply more motivated and energetic than others. Such children may not even need any external motivation to get moving and look for jobs.

It is also a good idea to start teaching your children about the tax system when they start working. Spend time explaining how paying taxes works and how tax brackets increase with earnings. Of course, taxes must be explained in an age-appropriate way. And I am fairly sure that I would certainly overwhelm my 6-year-old daughter with topics such as tax estimates or types of taxes (income, payroll, corporate, sales, etc.).

But at the very beginning I would do it like this:

Taxes are when the residents, like your mom and me, give money to the state. The state uses this money to carry out certain tasks. For example, the money is used for roads, kindergartens, schools, sports facilities, hospitals, and much more. In addition, the state pays the teachers, the police officers, and everyone else who works for the state with the taxes.

But why is it important to talk to kids about taxes?

When you discuss taxes with your children, they will gain a better understanding of their civic role as responsible citizens. It helps children understand that paying taxes is a means to support the community and ensure that public services are provided for the benefit of all.

Talking about taxes also introduces basic financial literacy concepts to your children. It prepares them learn about income, expenses, and how taxes are used to fund public services, preparing them for their future financial responsibilities.

Moreover, talking about taxes helps build empathy and social responsibility in your children. They can comprehend how taxes help fund programs that aid individuals and communities facing hardships, creating empathy and emphasizing the importance of helping those in need.

By talking about taxes with your children, you are teaching them about their position in society, financial literacy, and the significance of their efforts. It trains children to be aware and responsible citizens who appreciate the role of taxes in keeping society running smoothly and fairly.

RECAP

Children naturally start understanding money's importance early on, so parents should nurture this curiosity with simple financial lessons. Start by teaching basic money concepts, such as the value of different bills and coins, and the idea of money as a tool for exchange. Using the barter system can help explain the value of money in relatable terms.

Address children's misconceptions about ATMs by explaining that money is earned through work and saved in the bank. Use piggy banks to illustrate that you can only withdraw what you have saved.

Guide children on managing their first earnings from allowances or gifts. Encourage them to spend, save, invest, or share their money, allowing them to make mistakes and learn from them. Instill the principle of exchange, teaching that providing value is essential for receiving value in return.

For preteens and teenagers, part-time jobs offer practical lessons in financial responsibility and time management. Ensure these jobs complement, not replace, allowances. Evaluate your child's readiness for work based on their reliability, maturity, independence, and motivation. Early work experiences teach essential life skills and prepare them for future responsibilities.

Teach that while jobs provide income, real wealth comes from smart financial decisions and investments. Explain the power of compound interest and how investing can build wealth over time. Encourage balancing earning with other life responsibilities, ensuring financial success doesn't come at the expense of personal well-being and family time.

By guiding children through these stages of financial education, you help them build a strong foundation for managing money responsibly and achieving financial independence.

ALLOWANCES

Introducing the concept of allowances for children can be a complex decision for parents. There are a wide range of opinions on whether children should be paid for their contributions to the household or receive money unconditionally. The key is to strike a balance between teaching financial skills and instilling a sense of responsibility. The Institute of Child Psychology recommends involving children in chores from a young age, while others believe in separate systems for earning and allowance. Ultimately, the goal is to help your children develop healthy financial habits that will benefit them in the long run. In this chapter, we will explore different types of allowances and considerations for giving allowances to children of different age groups.

Should You Pay Your Children for Doing Chores?

There are generally two schools of thought on the topic of giving an allowance in exchange for the child doing age-appropriate chores:

- One tends to believe that parents should allow their children to earn money in exchange for doing chores.
- The second argues that children should not be paid for their contributions to the management of a home/family that they are part of. This group often says that money should be given to children when they need it or without any condition. More specifically, that it should be unrelated to doing house chores.

Like everything in life, each point of view has its advantages and disadvantages.

The Institute of Child Psychology based in Canada has a clear opinion on this topic. On an Instagram post they sum it up as follows: "We want you to STOP paying your children to do their chores."[37] And they claimed it for a good reason. Their statement is based on one of the longest-running development studies in history (the study was started in 1938 and continues to this day) which set out to determine if children benefit from doing chores. The answer is a clear yes, as the study proves that children benefit from chores. From their point of view, children can be expected to help in the household, and this should start at the age of 18 months, exactly when the desire to help and mimic their parents is strong.[38]

No matter what system the parent adopts, they should always remember that the goal is not to just give children money, it is to improve their children's financial skills and give them a head start in life.

Personally, I have had good experiences not tying allowance to conditions, chores, or behavior. Even if your child has misbehaved, you should not impose conditions such as withholding allowance until they clean their room. On the other hand, my wife and I believe that children should not be paid for everyday help around the house. As a family, we should all contribute to helping around the household. Children should not be paid for doing what is expected of them.

Below is a short overview with age-appropriate chores for children. (Please keep in mind that this list is not exhaustive and that chores may vary according to culture and origin.)

Ages 2 to 3:
Clean up toys
Put away books
Take clothes to laundry
Dispose of trash
(preferably in the trash can)
Fetch diapers and wipes
Dust baseboards

Ages 4 to 5:
Feed pets
Wipe up spills
Put away toys
Straighten bedroom
Sort clean silverware
Vacuum the floor
Clear kitchen table
Fold towels
Feed pets
Help with meal prep
Water plants

Ages 6 to 7:
Gather trash
Dust mop floors
Empty dishwasher
Match clean socks
Water garden plants
Rake leaves
Prepare simple snacks
Replace toilet paper roll

Ages 8 to 9:
Peel potatoes or carrots
Make salad
Load dishwasher
Wash laundry
Dust furniture
Put groceries away
Scramble eggs
Bake cookies
Walk dogs
Sweet porches
Wipe off table

Ages 10 to 11:
Clean bathroom
Vacuum
Clean countertops
Deep clean kitchen
Prepare easy meals
Mow lawn
Bring in mail
Take out trash
Clean fridge

Ages 12+:
Mop floors
Change overhead lights
Wash/vacuum car
Trim hedges
Paint walls
Shop for groceries (with a list)
Cook complete dinner
Bake bread or cake
Do simple home repairs
Wash windows
Iron clothes
Watch younger siblings

When I talk to parents about allowances, the first question is nearly always "How much should I give?" There are also countless recommendations on this, but it's important to find something that works for you.[39] I will go into more details in the next few paragraphs, but for me there is one basic principle: The amount of pocket money depends on the financial possibilities of the family and the age of the child.

Please also remember that the knowledge that "material things and money do not automatically make people happy" is an important foundation. Shared experiences with parents and siblings may have a longer lasting effect than the joy of a newly purchased toy.

In a family relationship, skills and values are imparted and practiced, creating a lasting impact on individuals. Within the family unit, various skills are developed and honed through daily interactions and activities. For example, children learn practical skills such as cooking, cleaning, and managing household chores, which are essential for their personal growth and independence. Additionally, values like honesty, respect, empathy, and responsibility are instilled within the family environment, shaping the character and moral compass of each family member.

The significance of these skills and values lies in their long-term influence. When practiced consistently within the family, they become ingrained in individuals' behaviors and attitudes, extending beyond the family unit and into other aspects of their lives. The skills acquired and the values internalized within the family relationship serve as a strong foundation for individuals to navigate their personal and professional lives, foster healthy relationships, and contribute positively to society.

To help my daughter understand that material and monetary things don't make you happy, we use a smiley list at home. The concept behind it is simple. Whenever our daughter does something particularly well or has behaved well, she gets a sticker showing a smiley. She can stick these on a sheet of paper and whenever a row is full of smiley faces, she gets to make a wish. We have 4 rows of 7 smileys each. (Theoretically, it takes 4 weeks to complete if it goes well, but experience shows that it is more likely to be 1.5 to 2 months.) In the beginning, my daughter always wanted us to buy a Paw Patrol magazine from the newsstand around the corner. Hence, we adjusted the system a bit. For the first three rows, she can decide what activity we do together. For example, a trip to the park, a walk to a special place, or a visit to the zoo. If the last row is filled with smileys, she gets the beloved Paw Patrol magazine.

This story is not to discourage you from giving an allowance to your child. However, it's to let you know that the allowance shouldn't be seen as a way to forcefully make them do things, since they want the money. It should rather be utilized as a tool for them to learn how to do things and develop habits that will keep growing even if they don't get their allowance anymore.

What Type of Allowance Should I Give?

Let me tell you a story. Jessica is a financial coach who got divorced one year after she got married. She said: "All I got out of my marriage was my beautiful daughter Anabelle and my clothes. I lost everything else because of how financially irresponsible my ex-husband was. It took me eight years to get my life together, and I promised myself that my daughter was going to be financially smart. I promised to teach her as much as possible. But this was not easy. I coach people about their finances for a living, but with my children, and with children generally—as I have come to learn—you must be careful and attentive. There is no one rule. Giving Anabelle allowances was not easy. I started one way and ended up doing something entirely different. I had to adjust to what would work for her instead of applying broad recommendations. Now, when people ask me whether they should give their children allowances, I just suggest that whatever system they choose to use should be tailored around who their child is. Know your child and observe what system is likely to have the best effect."

Whatever you do, do not give your children money out of guilt or as a substitution for your love and physical presence. Life is increasingly becoming more stressful, and people are being forced to sacrifice more than they want to for things they need. Unfortunately, many parents are being forced to sacrifice spending a good amount of time with their family in the hustle to make ends meet. Many more children are left at home and compensated with money. This is all part of what money teaches.

TYPES OF ALLOWANCES

Here are different types of allowance to choose from:

The "Payment for Chores" Allowance

This is the most widely recognized sort of allowance, however, don't forget to only do this once in a while, as I have shown above. I am not a big supporter of this allowance but will describe it for the sake of completeness. Children are expected to do certain tasks in the household in exchange for cash. In this scenario, there is a specific dollar amount tied to a specific task or tasks. The advantages are that the child will see an immediate connection between the work they do and the cash they get. For this to be viable, there should be ramifications when the errands are not done. This requires parents to follow through. If there are a few children in the family, that might also be expensive to manage. An option is to have a list of tasks that need doing with a set financial reward for each errand. You may require your children to select a various number of tasks or simply allocate each to them. More elaborate work pays more, while speedy or simple errands pay less. If your children do not accomplish the work, they should not receive the cash even if it's tempting to give it to them.

"No Conditions" Allowance

This method involves giving your children a particular amount regularly without them having to work for it.

This is advantageous because the children receive the allowance at a set date, either weekly or monthly, and they must learn to manage the given amount. It is like a salary. The children can make plans for the money—spending, saving, and other things. It is a good way to teach your children financial planning.

When implementing the "No Conditions" Allowance method, different schedules and age groups are recommended for several reasons. Varying schedules, such as weekly or monthly allowances, allow children to learn budgeting and financial responsibility at different stages of their development. Younger children benefit from shorter timeframes to manage their money and learn immediate consequences, while older children can handle longer-term planning. Age groups determine the appropriate amount of allowance, gradually increasing as children grow older and take on more responsibilities. Tailoring schedules and amounts according to age ensures age-appropriate financial lessons and helps children build the necessary skills to handle money responsibly as they mature.

The disadvantage is that this method does not teach your child that pay is compensation for a job well done. This is why I would generally recommend giving payment for them doing extra chores. Receiving money whether they do their chores or not isn't always a good character-building experience for children because they receive the money for free.

The Hybrid

The compromise between all these measures is a hybrid model. I have spoken to many parents over the years and this system seems to work for most of them.

This involves children doing regular chores in the house without payment, while they can also earn money from handling bigger responsibilities or more difficult tasks, like helping when painting the house or cleaning the basement and so on. You can discuss money with them and agree on a payment plan.

The disadvantage of this is that your children might not be interested in doing certain difficult chores, whether they are getting paid or not.

At this point in my manuscript, my editor always felt reminded of her childhood. She told me that she and her brother always had to clean their father's car. She said, "It never mattered how much he tried to bribe us, we hated washing the car and he couldn't ever get us to do it!" I can imagine this so well, and I would love to experience this situation live. It always reminds me of how much it bothered me when I had to sweep the street *again*. Of course, children have everything else on their mind and certainly this is not a clean and polished car.

That's where negotiation comes in. Don't forget that forcing children to do these things will often defeat the purpose. The goal is to incentivize them by rewarding them for their work. My wife and I have decided that our daughter will get her allowance as soon as she starts elementary school. There are many wonderful opportunities to learn how to be responsible, for example, when she wants to buy a refreshing drink or a healthy snack at the school kiosk.

Trial and Error

Don't be rigid. If one method does not seem to be giving you the desired result, try something new until you find what works. No system is foolproof, so do not beat yourself up too much when it does not go as planned. You've got this!

SHOULD YOU GIVE YOUR CHILDREN (AGES 5 TO 8) AN ALLOWANCE?

There have been arguments over the years amongst parents about whether it is advisable to give children of this age group (5 to 8) allowance.

My view is: Why not? It is not like you are giving them a large amount of money. Just enough to give them a taste of financial responsibility. Introduce them to the allowance system. You cannot try to bring up financially literate children without allowing them to handle money themselves. The earlier they start, the better it is for them.

With that in mind, how much is okay to give as an allowance to children within this age group? I suggest anywhere between $5 to $8, weekly or monthly (both time frames are fine). Now, different strokes for different folks, but whatever you go for, let it not be too low that it does not allow them to save and spend, and let it not be too high that they can't manage it. With this amount, you can walk them through using it to buy a candy bar or show them how it will accumulate if they put it in their piggy bank. If this is their first allowance, there is no need to go overboard; their needs are not so dire that you need to break the bank to give them an allowance. Remember, you are training them.

When you start the allowance, talk to them, and help them divide it into savings and spending. It is unwise to give your children an allowance without proper supervision. After all, if they're too young to understand the value, they might lose it! Let them know that their allowance is a constant in their lives at that point and for the foreseeable future, so they can plan.

HOW MUCH ALLOWANCE SHOULD YOU GIVE YOUR PRETEENS (AGES 9 TO 12)?

If your child returns home from school with anecdotes about how much their friends get for their allowance, consider this basic rule before discussing the amount you should give your children.

An overall dependable guideline is to pay $1 for each year of life, so an 8-year-old would get $8 a week, a 14-year-old $14 a week, etc. If this appears to be high (or low), you can decide on whatever appears to be sensible based on the chores your children take on (if you link their stipend to chores), the number of children you give an allowance to, what your financial capacity or plan is, and what sort of reward framework you use.

If a simple $5 or $10 per week (or even per month) sounds better to you than paying a dollar for each year of your child's age, go ahead and do it. The goal is to show your children how important cash is and teach them the value of it.

A basic three-container technique can be a viable way to help children with managing their cash and watch their saving and investment funds develop:

Get three enormous containers and mark them, respectively: *spending*, *saving*, and *good causes*. Older adolescents should be encouraged to set aside a portion of their cash for future needs.

As a parent, once you've set them up on the right path, resist the urge to monitor them consistently. Allow them to spend. Part of the training is permitting children to spend their cash on things they want. Children also need to discover that work brings rewards. With age comes more responsibility, and that incorporates being responsible for managing their cash flow. Preteens, especially those who earn money doing jobs like raking leaves, lawn mowing, or babysitting, should be encouraged to pay for themselves when they go to the movies or eat out with their friends. They may also be required to contribute to the family cellphone plan, or simply cover a portion of their expenses.

HOW MUCH ALLOWANCE SHOULD YOU GIVE TEENAGERS (AGES 13 TO 17)?

Experts around the world argue about how much allowance should be given, at what age, and with what frequency. The allowance of a teenager would generally be a minimum of $10 per week, however, you can decide how to give it to them, daily or weekly, depending on your finances as a parent. In my opinion, their allowance shouldn't be more than $100 a month. (I am aware that this is an astronomically high amount for many families. For this reason alone, it should not be exceeded.)

For children aged 9-12, I recommend a *monthly* allowance because it allows them to learn the fundamentals of budgeting. This structure encourages them to plan and manage their expenses over a longer period. Once they transition into their teenage years, it becomes advantageous to introduce more regular payments to reinforce their budgeting skills. By allowing teenagers to demonstrate their learned skills through consistent payments, they can further refine their financial management abilities and cultivate a sense of responsibility and independence. Keeping their allowance within $100 per month ensures a reasonable amount for their needs and encourages responsible spending habits.

YOUNG ADULTS (AGES 18 TO 21)

In my view, this age group shouldn't be entitled to an allowance anymore. By discontinuing the practice of providing an allowance, young adults are given an opportunity to learn important life skills and cultivate a strong work ethic, while taking ownership of their financial responsibilities. This shift encourages them to actively seek employment, explore career opportunities, or pursue higher education while also managing their own finances. It fosters a sense of self-reliance, resourcefulness, and adaptability that is crucial for their personal and professional development.

Moreover, by not relying on an allowance, young adults can gain valuable real-world experiences and learn to navigate financial challenges independently. They become more aware of budgeting, saving, and making financial decisions aligned with their goals and aspirations. This hands-on approach to money management instills a sense of financial maturity and prepares them for the financial realities of adulthood.

It is important to note that individual circumstances and cultural norms may influence the decision to provide or discontinue an allowance during this age group. Some parents may still choose to provide financial support or assistance based on specific circumstances, such as educational expenses or temporary financial difficulties. However, the underlying idea remains that encouraging young adults to make their own money promotes personal growth, responsibility, and self-sufficiency.

Synopsis

When considering how to teach kids about money, research shows that youngsters as young as age three may comprehend financial concepts such as currency counting. Many of their financial behaviors become engrained by the age of seven.

Therefore, educating your children about money management at a young age makes the most sense.

You want to encourage and nourish the money-related inquiries they ask. When doing so, make certain that you complement these with age-appropriate replies that do not go over their heads.

Consider initiating more involved money conversations around the age of five or six, though children grow at various speeds. When the questions begin to pile up, offer them easy access to your financial knowledge and praise them when they make wise decisions.

Average Allowance for Children by Age

One commonly acknowledged rule of thumb is to give children between $1 and $2 every week, depending on their age. So, if you had a six and a nine-year-old, you may pay them $6 and $9, respectively. However, offering a youngster a bigger allowance based solely on his or her age is not always justified.

According to RoosterMoney, here's a brief comparison of weekly allowance ranges for children aged four to fourteen[40]:

- 4-year-olds – $4.18
- 5-year-olds – $4.79
- 6-year-olds – $5.82
- 7-year-olds – $7.42
- 8-year-olds – $8.01
- 9-year-olds – $8.71
- 10-year-olds – $9.49
- 11-year-olds – $10.43
- 12-year-olds – $11.91
- 13-year-olds – $12.62
- 14-year-olds – $13.87

Since younger children are not yet practiced in allocating money over a longer period of time, it is advisable to hand out pocket money on a weekly basis. As they get older and more experienced, the amounts can be paid monthly.

Note: Regardless of my recommendation, it is crucial that the pocket money fits into the family budget.

RECAP

Introducing allowances to children involves finding a balance between teaching financial skills and instilling a sense of responsibility. Opinions differ on whether allowances should be tied to chores or given unconditionally. The goal is to help children develop healthy financial habits.

Two main views exist. One supports paying children for chores to teach the value of work, while the other advocates for giving money unconditionally, believing chores are a family responsibility. Both approaches have their merits and drawbacks.

The Institute of Child Psychology advises against tying allowances to chores, suggesting children should help around the house from an early age without monetary incentives.

Children should gradually take on more complex tasks as they age. For example, children ages 2-3 can clean up toys and dispose of trash, ages 4-5 can feed pets and fold towels, ages 6-7 can empty the dishwasher and rake leaves, ages 8-9 can make salad and scramble eggs, ages 10-11 can clean the bathroom and prepare easy meals, and ages 12+ can cook complete dinners and do simple home repairs.

The amount of the allowance should fit the family's financial situation and the child's age. A common rule is to give $1 per year of the child's age per week. Adjust this based on what works best for your family.

Types of allowances include payment for chores, which encourages a work ethic but may lead to entitlement; no conditions allowance, which teaches budgeting but doesn't link money to work; and the hybrid model, which combines both approaches, rewarding extra tasks while maintaining family responsibilities.

Introduce allowances at a young age to foster financial literacy. Help children divide their allowance into spending, saving, and charitable giving. As children grow older, encourage them to take on more financial responsibilities and budget for their own expenses.

By ages 18-21, young adults should transition away from allowances, encouraging financial independence through employment and real-world financial management.

Start financial education early, tailor the allowance system to your child's needs, and adjust as they grow. This approach fosters financial literacy, responsibility, and independence.

SAVING & INVESTING

> *If saving money is wrong, I don't want to be right!*
>
> – William Shatner

Saving involves teaching children about delayed gratification, which is keeping aside money that they can spend in the future.

Delayed gratification is not a term that everyone is used to or particularly enjoys. Some adults have not even come to terms with the concept of not spending all they have at once, so we need to be extremely patient with children. They will probably have questions about savings and why it is a necessity. Be ready with your answer.

Guide and encourage your children to save. As I have said, many adults do not find saving enjoyable (though some other parents may love it) because delayed gratification is not something that is remotely appealing to them. Just imagine how children feel about it then. The many statistics about how poorly we have collectively done with saving is proof that it is a difficult task for most. According to a Bankrate.com survey, which asked 1,000 working-class Americans about the amount set aside for emergencies or retirement from their annual income, some are not saving at all. In fact, 20% of those who save only save 5% or less of their income, while 28% save 6-10% of their income. Just 16 % are saving more than 15% of their income.

So, we must be patient with our children as we help them build a healthy saving culture. You might have to go the extra mile to encourage them to save, especially when they are preteens, with many things calling their attention to spend money on. Especially with the influx of social media, fast shipping, instant pay, and a stream of never-ending advertisements. Children are more inundated than ever with the urge to buy what they want, when they want it.

It is crucial for your child to develop a sense of comfort with saving from a young age. I've come to understand this truth through my own personal experiences and the experiences shared by others. Often, we tend to forget the valuable lessons we've learned over time. However, for young adults who are still striving to find their balance and reduce dependence on their parents, this challenge can be even more significant. As they may have secured a part-time job or be actively seeking one, they find themselves shouldering greater responsibilities.

In this transitional phase of life, it is amazingly easy to forget the importance of savings. The pressure of life might force them to live from paycheck to paycheck. As an adult, you have passed this stage of life and have had these experiences in your own time, so it is your responsibility to look out for them and ensure they are still on track.

Doing without, setting priorities

Please always keep in mind that in the first years of school, there is often a big gap between wishful thinking and reality. It is understandable that children at this age have little idea of the cost or amount of things they want. They first must learn that they cannot have everything they want.

Having discussions with your child about prioritizing and delayed gratification is crucial for their understanding and development. Here's an example of how you can approach this conversation:

Parent: "You know, I've noticed that sometimes we can't have everything we want. Do you remember when you wanted that new toy, but we couldn't buy it right away?"

Child: "Yes, I remember."

Parent: "Exactly. Sometimes, there are other things we need to take care of first, like paying for groceries or bills. We must make choices about how we spend our money. It's important to prioritize our needs over our wants. It doesn't mean we'll never get what we want, but we might have to wait a little longer."

Child: "But why do we have to wait?"

Parent: "That's a great question! Waiting helps us appreciate things even more when we finally get them. It also teaches us the value of patience and the importance of saving for something we really want. For example, if you save your allowance for a few weeks, you can buy that toy you've been wanting. It's like a special reward for being patient and making a plan."

Child: "Oh, I see. So, I can't have everything I want right away?"

Parent: "Exactly. Learning to prioritize and make choices is an important skill. It helps us make wise decisions and be responsible with our money. We can still have fun and enjoy the things we want, but it's good to understand that sometimes we have to wait and be patient."

Child: "I'll try to be patient and save my money then!"

Parent: "That's fantastic! I'm proud of you for understanding. Let's make a wish list together, and you can decide which items are most important to you. We can work on saving money for those special things, and you'll feel great when you achieve your goals!"

Remember, every child is different, so adapt the conversation to their age and comprehension level. Encourage questions and keep the dialogue open to foster their understanding of financial responsibility.

When dealing with money, different behaviors become apparent. There are children who spend their money easily, while others are more frugal. You may even see different behaviors between the oldest and youngest child. One way to get everyone on the same page is to introduce your child to a wish list. With the help of a wish list, your child may find out which wish is the most important and begin to prioritize. In between, you can always ask if their wish list is still current or if something has changed.

EMERGENCY FUNDS

Unfortunately, many adults don't have emergency funds. Too many families across the world are one accident, emergency, or diagnosis away from losing everything they have. This is why it's imperative to teach your child about emergency funds. Like all people, they need a buffer to take them through the curve balls life is throwing at them and in the future once they've stepped into the reality of life. An emergency fund is a perfect buffer.

As the name suggests, an emergency fund is simply money one sets aside for life's unexpected events. It is your safety net, something to help you through a major life crisis. An emergency fund makes it possible for your child to go through life's major problems easily.

> *Do not save what is left after spending
> but spend what is left after saving.*
>
> – Warren Buffet

However, this knowledge does not seem to be widespread. A survey conducted in the US in 2021 showed that 25% of respondents did not have an emergency fund. The number increased by 4% compared to the previous year. Additionally, 26% of respondents reported having an emergency fund, but not enough to pay for three months of expenses.[41] A bankrate study came to a similarly shocking conclusion, since "only 39% of Americans have enough to cover a $1,000 unexpected expense."[42]

And what are my experiences? Well, emergency funds have saved me on several occasions. One example is when I moved to Switzerland, I was running short of money and my budget was tight. (The cost of living in Switzerland is many times higher than in Germany.) Then I got into what could have been a big problem for me: I backed into a car. It was not just a slight scratch—the door of the other car I crashed into was bent, and the car was in a terrible state. The good news was that nobody was hurt. The bad news was that it was going to cost me a lot of money that I did not have back then. It would have been a terrible situation for me if it hadn't been for my emergency fund.

Emergency funds are meant for all kinds of accidents and charges that insurance won't cover. It will save your children through emergency events like hospital visits, car accidents, etc. While talking to them about emergency funds, it is important to draw lines on what an emergency is and what it is not. This brings up the necessity to cover lessons about needs and wants, bearing in mind all needs are not always emergencies.

An emergency is something unexpected that, when not tackled immediately, would threaten your life, or has the potential to cost you a large amount of money you haven't budgeted for. Things like getting on a flight for a wedding are not an emergency. Things like getting a car or an extremely expensive gift for your partner are not an emergency. It is important your draw the lines on what emergencies are.

Nobody knows what turn life will take next, and I am sure you do not want to leave your children at the mercy of unforeseen circumstances. With emergency funds, your children will be able to tackle life's problems without relying on credit cards or high-interest loans. An emergency fund is also a vital step towards being debt-free, as it can prevent your children from borrowing money to solve problems. Finding a way not to get into further debt is an important step towards being debt-free.

HOW MUCH SHOULD YOUR CHILDREN SAVE?

When it comes to teaching your children about saving money, it's important to establish clear guidelines that suit their individual circumstances. If they are not currently facing any financial burdens, they have the freedom to decide on the amount they wish to save. Let them start small, for example, with $500 at the age of 13 to 17. This allows them to save a considerable sum for themselves at a young age.

Financial literacy expert, Beth Kobliner, in her book "Make Your Kid a Money Genius" suggests that children should strive to save at least 10% to 15% of their income or allowance. This practice instills the habit of saving and sets the groundwork for responsible financial management in the future.[43]

Encourage them to consider their short-term and long-term goals and determine a savings target that aligns with their aspirations.

A good rule of thumb in emergency funds says to have enough savings to cover a year's worth of expenses or at least three to six months' worth of expenses. (I prefer a year as I want to keep my family safe and cover all unexpected occasions.)

It is important that you encourage your children to save a portion of their money, but also allow them the freedom to spend some on things they truly value and enjoy. This balanced approach helps children understand the importance of saving while still experiencing the rewards of their efforts.

Regardless of your children's specific situation, the importance of building an emergency fund cannot be overstated. (No matter how old you are and what situation you are in, your emergency fund must be well filled. It is your safety net.) Hence, encourage your kids to start saving as soon as possible, emphasizing the significance of setting aside a portion of their income regularly. This habit will lay a strong foundation for their financial well-being and equip them with the necessary tools to navigate unforeseen circumstances in the future.

Where Should Your Child Keep Their Emergency Fund?

Many people make the wrong choice here. Do not just allow your children to put their emergency funds anywhere. Emergencies can happen on short notice. Therefore, don't tie up an emergency fund in a long-term investment account from which they will have trouble withdrawing it.

They should put it in an accessible account, but also ensure they do not put in the same account used for daily financial activities so as not to be tempted to use it. The best place to put an emergency fund is a high-yield savings account (although the interest rate level is not particularly attractive at the moment) or an ETF savings plan (however, the latter often needs at least 2 or 3 days for the money to become available). A savings account is a safe place to keep emergency funds because, in the United States for instance, it has federal insurance of up to $250,000. The money also earns interest and can be easily withdrawn or transferred to another account to be used immediately.

INVESTING

> *Compound interest is the eighth wonder of the world.*
> *He who understands it, earns it ... he who doesn't ... pays it.*
>
> – Albert Einstein*

There's no doubt that money management is the first step to learning how to save and invest. So, if you want to teach your children about investing money, the first important step is to let them know how to manage money.

Although a savings account is the best way to get kids to save, they can only scale money if they invest the money they earn. That is because children possess an immensely powerful gift which is time. The earlier your children start investing their money, the higher their returns will be. That's due to the power of compound interest. Compound interest is interest earned on interest added to capital, which thus earns interest again at the applicable interest rate along with the capital. If interest amounts are immediately reinvested or accumulated, the compound interest effect occurs: The invested capital grows faster, since interest paid out immediately earns interest again. Children love to experiment, and investments allow them the opportunity, with your guidance of course.

---

* Although this quote is regularly attributed to Einstein, I have not found any reliable proof that he really made this statement. My guess is that from a Marketing perspective a quote from Albert Einstein generates attention. Which works well. And frankly, the quote hits the mark.

The sooner you start educating your children, the more time they get to learn, make inquiries, and make mistakes in a protected and controlled environment. Furthermore, if you figure out how to do it properly and do it well, it can make life simpler.

In 2017, BusyChildren collaborated with Stockpile to turn into the leading chore/stipend broker that permits children to use their rewards to buy real stock on the stock market. Today 45,000 children are using the broker service.

"We target children aged 5 to 15," said BusyChildren CEO Gregg Murset. "That decade is the most critical to show children and establish a decent framework for them. In the wake of showing your children not to lie and cheat, cash abilities are the best things we can give them since this sets them up for a better future."[44] (Of course, this statement should be taken with a grain of salt. Because it is still true that children can only invest independently when they have reached the age of maturity.)

Murset is an experienced financial organizer and leading promoter for good parenting, children's responsibility, and financial proficiency. A father of six, he relates the steps his two younger children are making in the realm of stocks: "One of my children purchased Disney stock since he loves Disney films; the other purchased Ford since he prefers pickup trucks. The two of them precisely know the thing they are investing in, precisely what price they got it at, the two of them understand what their benefit is, or drawback is, and they like to focus on it themselves, which I think is incredible. If you can begin at an early age, you truly start something inside them that will lead to good habits later." Murset added: "Envision what they will be able to do if they own stocks and start putting effort in growing it."

He warns however that pushing your children to save or put money into something they aren't enthusiastic about is "an exercise in futility. I let them put resources into something they care about, or they believe is cool."

SAVING GOALS FOR KIDS (AGES 5 TO 8)

> *Not wasting money is the best way to save money.*
>
> – Mokokoma Mokhonoan

Setting goals can be fun for children especially when they are saving for something they want to do or love. You may have to model this for them.

For example, say you are saving to make a big purchase, like a new car, and your child wants something now or wonders why you are not doing something you would usually do, like eating out. You can talk to your child and explain that you are saving up to buy a car and that is why you will not spend money on eating out for now—delayed gratification. When your children set goals, especially when it is the first time, gauge how realistic it is for them to meet their target and if you can support them in achieving it. Doing this prevents them from being discouraged.

Get your child a piggy bank for their next birthday or holiday gift. In a world increasingly moving towards cashless societies, physical piggy banks may seem outdated. However, they still hold significant value for teaching children about saving, and they offer a tangible and interactive experience, allowing children to visualize their savings and develop financial habits.

I know a parent who worked with his 5-year-old to create a piggy bank out of used tins. The fact that they created it together made the child eager to save. The father said if he had known that working on the piggy bank together would have this effect on a child's enthusiasm for saving, he would have tried it with his other children when they were younger.

Whatever type of piggy bank you choose to use, whether you choose to create it alongside your children or buy it, the benefit of having it is the same. Since bank accounts or having digital savings are currently not available to children that age, a piggy bank is the best bet.

If their income comes from their allowance, birthdays, or cash from the tooth fairy, so will their savings. Let them decide how much to save from their income and then you do the math with them to make them aware of how much they would have saved after a period. Children at this stage require a lot of guidance but be sure to give them some room to make their own mistakes.

Play the Game "If I Could Make a Wish"

"If I Could Make a Wish" is a creative and imaginative game where players take turns sharing their wishes. Each wish builds upon the previous one, creating a chain of interconnected wishes. The game encourages imagination, storytelling, and discussions about personal desires and aspirations. There are no strict rules, allowing players to freely express their wishes and engage in imaginative storytelling.

This game provides an excellent opportunity to understand your child's deepest desires. Plus, thinking about realistic and unrealistic wishes is fun. Don't just listen, also tell them what you would like to have and why you have not yet or will never fulfill certain wishes. Saving is easier when you have a clear goal in mind. In this, children are no different from adults. Help your child find ways to achieve goals. Find out together whether money is needed to achieve these goals or what prerequisites must be met. define suitable savings goals with your child depending on his or her age. If a savings goal seems worthwhile to your child, he or she is more likely to be able to resist temptations.

Help your child save for what he or she has wished for. With this, everything will naturally fall in place and won't require as much effort or upkeep.

To avoid disappointment, it is worth checking whether the savings goal can be achieved in the allotted time. Your child will only be willing to save his or her money if the end goal can be achieved in a timely manner. Help your child check in on the savings goal by scheduling times in the calendar together. This will help keep the savings goals current. Perhaps by then the new computer game will no longer be as important, and the new bicycle is more desirable; consider together whether the savings goal should be changed, or the time horizon adjusted.

HOW TO HELP PRETEENS (AGES 9 TO 12) START SAVING AND INVESTING

> *10 years from now, your kids will be eating or starving from the decisions you have made today.*
>
> – Credit Medics

Discuss Wants vs. Needs

The initial phase in showing children the benefit of saving is to assist them with separating needs and wants. Clarify that necessities are food, housing, and clothing, and explain that anything outside the basic human necessities are only additional things. You can use your own financial plan as an illustration. Show them how wants should take a secondary place to necessities when money is tight. One of the fundamental principles of saving is that you should not have a lifestyle that's beyond your means.

Set Aside a Particular Spot/Place to Store Their Cash

As children accumulate savings, they will need a place to store their money. For young children, this might be a mini-safe, or you might need to set them up with a piggy bank. That way, they can see how their reserve funds are adding up and how much progress they are making towards their goal.

Have Them Track Their Spending

Becoming a better saver includes knowing where your cash is going. If your children get a reward, having them record their incomings and expenses every day and add them up toward the week's end can be an educational exercise. Urge them to consider how they are spending and how much quicker they could reach their saving goals if they changed their spending habits. If your child is old enough to use technology, encourage them to explore budgeting apps on your smartphone or theirs.

Set Reserve Fund Objectives

To a child, being advised to save—without being told *why*—may not make sense, especially if your child has the urge to spend. Assisting children with defining a saving or investment goal can be a better approach to convince them of why they should do it. Once they understand what it is they are putting something aside for, help them separate their objectives into reasonable steps. If they want to buy a $130 mini laptop and receive a $10 remittance every week, help them figure out how to get to their goal while keeping the money they're saving in mind.

Offer Reserve Fund Motivators

One reason people save through their company's retirement plan is that the organization is coordinating it. In case you are having trouble convincing your children to save, you can see how you can assist them in planning for it. If your child has defined a major savings goal—for instance, they want to buy a $500 iPad —you could offer to assist them in coordinating their savings efforts, like taking parts of their allowance and saving it for them daily or monthly. As another option, you could offer a prize when your children reach a saving milestone—for example, a $50 reward for hitting their midway point.

Leave Space for Slip-ups

A big part of putting children in charge of their cash is allowing them to learn from their blunders. It is enticing to step in and steer them away from a possibly expensive slip-up, however, it may be wiser to use this as a teachable moment. As a result, they'll know how to avoid making the same mistake in the future.

For instance, imagine your child wants to purchase a trendy toy that he has been eyeing for weeks. As a parent, you may be aware that the toy is overpriced and likely to lose its appeal quickly. It can be tempting to intervene and dissuade them from buying it. However, instead of preventing the purchase outright, you could have a conversation with your child about the toy's cost and potential alternatives. By allowing him to proceed with the purchase and experience the disappointment when the toy loses its allure, he will learn firsthand about making thoughtful spending choices. This valuable lesson will empower your child to consider the long-term value of their purchases and avoid similar impulsive buying decisions in the future.

Become Their Lender

A great way to teach your child the power of borrowing and debt is through lending with a small purchase. If your child has something they want to purchase and are eager to put money aside for it, turning into your children's lender can help them with an important exercise in saving. Assume your child needs to buy something for $80. You can offer to loan them the cash and request they pay back in installments from the allowance you give them, with interest. The lesson they should learn is that saving may mean postponing gratification for a little longer, but if they decide to borrow the money to have it now, the thing they want to buy will end up costing more.

How to Introduce Children to Savings Accounts

Here are the main things to cover when introducing the concept of saving accounts to your children:

Choosing How Much to Save

There are two unique themes to cover here. The first is choosing the amount to put aside for their individual goals, bearing in mind how long they have to reach their goal and the amount they can save week by week or month to month. The second is saving in case of emergencies.

Just remember what I already told you about emergency funds. Talk to your children about why having a backup savings plan is important and separate the mechanics of what you saved to reach the desired sum. This will help them avoid resorting to credit cards or asking for an advance.

Saving for Short Vs. Long-Term Goals

Teaching children about defining financial objectives matters for two reasons:

- It can help them understand the concept of saving cash for a reason. Setting aside cash just to save it can lose its appeal when you do not have a plan for using that cash eventually. What's more, we're all more likely to plunge into reserve funds when those dollars and pennies aren't reserved for a particular outcome.

- Defining objectives is also an inspiration to proceed with the reserve fund goal. It can help children understand concepts like delayed gratification and the contrast between needs and wants, both in the short and long haul.

Discuss with your children the importance of saving money for both small purchases, such as a dollar store toy, and larger purchases, such as a computer game. If they want to save money for more than one thing, assist them in opening separate savings accounts if your bank allows it. As a result, they can have various "pots" to allot investment funds to as they work towards their goals.

When encouraging children to open a bank account, it's important to highlight the benefits of "high-yield savings accounts" and how they can help grow their savings faster through interest. Point out that high-return bank accounts commonly offer higher rates than standard bank accounts. It very well may be useful to run a few instances of how much interest they could accrue in a year with an ordinary bank account versus a high-return one. But as mentioned earlier, the current level of interest rates is unattractive for long-term wealth accumulation. In particular, rising inflation rates may even cause money to depreciate faster than it earns interest. In my opinion, therefore, exchange-traded funds and the associated savings plans offer an attractive investment opportunity that currently has no alternative.

Talk About Savings Regularly

Encouraging children to save is not something you do once. It is an ongoing conversation that ought to progress and evolve as they get older and more experienced.

Four Different Ways to Get Your Preteens Acquainted With Investing

1. Explore investing as a family and share the keys to long-term rewards. Work with children to pick stock from organizations whose business models they understand and whose products they use. Urge them to research the companies to understand what they do. Together, take a look at their portfolio now and evaluate how it may change later.
2. Teach them that investing is all about the long haul. Urge children to put away only cash that they do not require for the time being. Offer stories and books about effective long-haul financial stock traders.
3. Start small and learn from mistakes. Show children the impact of investing, starting with a small amount of cash, so they can make mistakes and learn from them without it costing an enormous amount.
4. Make it important. At the point when children begin earning or getting cash—regardless of whether it's from allowances, a job, or chores—urge them to invest a portion of it, since it will help them build a solid financial basis for saving and investing.

I am a huge supporter of Exchange Traded Funds (ETFs). With them, you can easily and cheaply invest in stocks and accumulate assets over time. An ETF replicates the performance of well-known market indices (such as the SP 500). In essence, ETFs combine the benefits of stocks and funds into a single product at a low cost, resulting in higher long-term returns.

PRACTICAL STEPS TO TEACH YOUR TEENAGERS (AGES 13 TO 17) SAVING AND INVESTING

As kids enter their teenage years, it becomes more important for them to save. They not only have more earning potential, but their life expenses are often higher. For example, there are more opportunities to go out with friends, go on dates, and save for bigger purchases such as clothes, gas, or a car. Plus, if you have given them more financial responsibility, it may also get them to take savings more seriously.

Adolescence is also when talks about the future become more regular and important. It is time to start saving not just to buy games or go out and have fun, it is time to save for longer-term purposes, for more significant expenses like college tuition, getting a car, etc.

Saving for College

College is likely to be important to them at this age. Get to know the college your children would like to attend and encourage them to start saving towards it. You should make an estimated budget together of what it might cost to go to college, then put down realistic saving expectations, taking into consideration how much your children earn. When you have considered all that needs to be considered, finalize saving goals and monitor their progress.

Teaching your children to save up for college is an important lesson even if you plan to take care of all their college expenses. It teaches them the wisdom of controlling their appetite for wants to focus on what they need. They might have been saving for other things but probably not for something as big and as important as college. One of the most valuable pieces of financial intelligence you can teach your children is the ability to handle and execute financial plans, and it all starts with knowing how to set financial goals toward something important. It is a valuable financial lesson that no children this age should miss.

Of course, while teaching them to save towards college, you must be open with them. Let them know how much you can afford, and how much of what you can afford will go to them. Discuss the actual amount with them. Then also roll out another plan you have for taking care of their college funds aside from their savings. This will help make your children confident.

As you guide your children in saving for college, it's a good opportunity to also address the topic of student debt. Student loans have become a trendy way to fund higher education, and understanding the implications of borrowing money is critical for making informed decisions. Conversations regarding student debt help your children understand the long-term consequences of borrowing for college.

It is critical that you emphasize the potential difficulties involved with loan repayment, such as monthly payments, interest accumulation, and the impact on their financial future. To reduce the need for loans and the weight of debt after graduation, emphasize the necessity of investigating scholarships, grants, and other types of financial aid. You enable your children to examine alternate solutions and take proactive efforts to reduce their dependency on loans by highlighting the impact of student debt.

Encourage the creation of realistic goals that consider the costs of tuition, books, living expenses, and other related expenses.

Explore tactics for increasing their savings together, as well as prospective part-time employment, internships, or work-study possibilities that might add to their college fund while providing useful experiences. You can encourage good financial planning in your children by adding discussions about student debt into the dialogue about saving for college.

Taking Fear Out of Money Discussions

Never sound fearful when talking about money with your children, even when you are being honest and realistic. Communicating fear will easily stick in their head and they might become scared of anything related to money.

Fearing money is a leading factor in becoming poor and making money mistakes. Having the right money mindset is yet another core part of the financial literacy lesson you must instruct your children.

Setting Saving Goals and Maintaining Discipline

When it comes to saving money, it's important to instill the value of setting goals and maintaining discipline. While saving for college is a significant aspect of the financial journey, there are other important things for which to save. By teaching the same logic that applies to saving for college, you can empower your child to prioritize financial goals and develop a sense of responsibility.

Imagine your child wants to buy a car. This presents a perfect opportunity to have an open discussion about the details and responsibilities involved. Talk about who will cover the cost of the car itself, as well as the ongoing expenses like maintenance, insurance, and gas. By involving them in these discussions, you can foster a sense of ownership and encourage your child to create a comprehensive saving plan tailored to their specific goals.

As your child works towards these goals, keep a close eye on the progress and offer guidance and support when needed. This approach not only helps to develop discipline but also cultivates a sense of pride and accomplishment as your child will witness their savings grow according to the plan.

Ways to Teach Your Teenagers to Save

Here are some suggestions for teaching your children to save money at this age:

1. *Reemphasize the difference between needs and wants:* This is the very foundation of saving. Children must always bear in mind that not every expense is necessary. Most children find it difficult to learn this vital lesson of delayed gratification, which is why it's important to reinforce this concept often.

    One of the ways you can teach them the difference is to make them write down their needs according to their order of importance or scale of preference. It can help if you show them with your own needs and wants so they can see how you make sacrifices and choices between the two. Additionally, when they come to you for money, deliberately do not solve everything at once by giving them the money for it, even if you can at that moment. Delay their gratification for some time before you then meet the need. But what does that mean exactly?

    It means that you intentionally postpone the immediate fulfillment of your child's desire or request for something he or she wants. Instead of immediately providing the money or fulfilling the desire, you purposefully create a waiting period or delay before meeting the need or want.

By delaying gratification, you are teaching your child the value of patience, self-control, and the ability to prioritize. It helps children understand that not every desire or want can be instantly fulfilled and that waiting and saving for something can bring greater satisfaction overall.

2. *Teach them about taxes and accounting:* At this age, your child may be making their way into the working world gradually, so this is the right time to teach them all about taxes, the difference between gross pay and net pay, etc.

If you prefer preparing your taxes online with the help of software, you can also teach your children by fully involving them in the process and showing them how the whole thing works. Show them how the software works and explain why you use the one you use. If there later is a need for a change in your tax software or your process, let your children know.

Just make sure you familiarize them with all the financial tools you use to plan your taxes and household finances. If you leave the planning of your household finances to the hands of a professional or certified financial adviser or planner, your children might not be able to learn the process from you, so you must involve them each time you have a meeting with your planner. This would open them up to the essentials of accounting and planning household finances and taxes.

Being open and transparent like this will help your children learn a lot and help them develop an interest in handling financial matters well.

3. *Be their creditor:* Children may not be wired to live within their means. We sometimes must let them realize their mistakes first. That's why we shouldn't just jump in to help. But once we can see that they have indeed learned from their mistakes, the right thing is obviously to help them out.

Simply imagine the following situation: Your child repeatedly spends all his/her allowance on unnecessary items and faces the consequences of not having enough money for something important, such as a school event or a desired purchase. If you notice that he or she has genuinely learned from this experience, demonstrating improved decision-making and responsible spending, then it is appropriate to step in and offer guidance or assistance when needed.

Peer pressure is often at the root of the urgency to buy. Social media and social comparison leave children wanting to be like another child or wanting whatever another child has without considering the difference in affordability. At this stage, your children are looking for their voice and seeking genuine expression and independence but, at the same time, they are scared and in need of acceptance and a sense of belonging. This makes them more vulnerable to peer pressure.

While there's no escaping peer pressure, you can still teach your child a valuable lesson. Let me show you how.

For example, as we saw before, if they are impatient about getting an item that costs $100, lend them the money and demand repayment plus interest from the allowance you give them or what they earn at work. They might end up paying you $150. And they will realize that they have spent $50 extra for the item they wanted.

As simple as this lesson looks, it forms the very tenet of saving. It also teaches the consequences of bad debt. This lesson will be useful to your children throughout their lives.

4. *Offer saving incentives:* As said before, how many parents would be saving with their employer's retirement plan if there was no company matching contribution? I feel the answer would be none. After all, who doesn't want free money?

   If you want your child to have a saving goal of $200 a year, for instance, offer to match a percentage of that $200. You could also set milestones for your child as he or she embarks on their saving journey. Offer a reward for every milestone they reach. (For instance, a $20 bonus for reaching the halfway point.)

5. *Teach them to track their spending:* How many children keep track of how much they spend each week? Very few of them. A major part of saving is keeping track of spending. Chances are your child doesn't know how much they spend simply living or having fun—going out with friends to see movies, play games, and do other fun and frivolous things. They only become aware of their money when they are almost broke or going broke.

Helping them track their spending could be a revelation to how much they can save from their allowances and earnings. Create an agreement together and then have them list their purchases every day and sum it up at the end of the week to see just how much they have spent and what they spent on. Review this together and discuss accordingly.

Steps for Investing

If I could be a teenager again, the first financial decision I would make would be to invest my money wisely. I cannot go back in time, but I can teach my daughter instead how to invest her money. Your child should have heard the word 'investing' repeatedly by now if you've been discussing money with them, but they might not have understood what it means to invest or how to go about it, so you must teach them.

They should know the basics of investing, what it means to put money in and get money back. If they are looking for ways to increase their earnings, and they know there is no independence without money, they will start thinking about investing their money too.

Try Out an Index Fund

I was discussing with a colleague how difficult it is to teach teens to invest their money.

While tech stocks might be a new thing for teenagers, you should also try to point them in the direction of index funds or ETFs as I have mentioned before.

What are index funds?

An index fund is a type of mutual fund that makes investing easy and profitable. It helps investors build a diverse portfolio that holds different assets, such as stocks, bonds, and commodities.

The main benefits of index funds

Investing all your money into one stock or company is a risky thing to do. You are left at the mercy of one company because, if the company fails, you will lose all your investment. You can easily reduce the risk of investment by splitting your money between different assets. The risk is reduced, for example, when you split your investment across different companies because when one company fails or goes bankrupt, you will not lose all your money.

It is not easy to diversify investments. Buying a single stock can cost hundreds of dollars, so purchasing multiple shares in different companies might cost tens of thousands or even millions of dollars. Few people can afford the money for such an investment.

An index fund solves this problem, as it focuses on tracking specific market indexes. Index funds like the ones that map the S&P 500 are meant to represent a broad swath of the market. S&P index funds alone represent the 500 largest companies in the United States. The Russell 2000 keeps a tab on 2,000 small publicly traded companies. Index funds are safer than actively managed funds that try to outperform and win over the market. Unlike actively managed funds, the index simply follows the market. For instance, if the S&P 500 gains 15% in a year, S&P index funds aim to also gain the same 15%. It does the same with a loss. If the S&P 500 loses 5% in a year, the index funds will also lose 5%.

Index funds have another advantage over actively managed funds; they have lower expense ratios than actively managed funds. (There are also actively managed index funds! Seriously? I think this is an advertising gimmick by the investment companies, so they can collect higher fees. An index is static and rarely changes, so there is nothing to be actively managed.) This is primarily because index funds are easy to manage and do not require as much input and decision-making from fund managers as active funds do. The managers of actively managed funds must make decisions about which stocks to buy and sell. Customers' requests to buy and sell shares are handled by fund managers. At the same time, they maintain a share allocation that allows the mutual fund to track its target index precisely.

An index fund is a better investment strategy than actively managed funds because, at the end of the day, the market is unbeatable. It is programmed to always win. You could pay all the high ratio fees and still not have great returns on your investment. Index funds offer better returns on investment, in case you are not an investment professional who knows how to actively manage your portfolio and is willing to spend time on investment research and selection.

To be fair, there are a few fund managers who have consistently outperformed the market over time. To invest with them, however, you'd need several millions of dollars. As a result, this is not a viable method of accumulating wealth.

Why are index funds good for your children?

1. *It is an easy investment:* Index funding is a simple investment. Neither you nor your children must have a lot of knowledge of stocks and how to manage investments.

All you must do is choose a fund provider to buy shares from. Look at the ones that have the best total expense ratios (TER). With index funds, it is easy to build a diversified portfolio for your children without spending a lot. For a start, they can buy one stock-focused fund or a fund focused on bonds. As time goes on and they have more savings or begin to earn more, they can also include international stocks and bonds.

2. *Low cost:* Index funds are cheap. You cannot find any better or cheaper ways to invest in the stock market. It has a total expense ratio of 0.12%. If your child invests $1,000, they will only have to pay $1.20. Brokers also do not charge much to buy or sell stocks compared to other investment types. A typical index fund broker will charge around $3 for each transaction. If you pay that over 50 different companies on your fund portfolio, you would be paying $150.

Most brokers do not charge anything if you are investing in their index funds. There are those who don't charge much either. And you only must pay the commission once instead of paying multiple times. This saves you a lot of money.

STEPS ON HOW YOUNG ADULTS (AGES 18 TO 21) CAN START BUILDING WEALTH

As our children reach maturity, it becomes increasingly important for us as parents to continue guiding and supporting them as they pursue financial independence. The transition from youth to early adulthood provides a once-in-a-lifetime opportunity to instill lasting savings and wealth-building behaviors. In this section, we will look at practical strategies that parents can share with their young adult children, ages 18 to 21, to help them build a solid financial foundation. We empower them to calculate their savings objectives, design a monthly savings strategy, embrace the value of change, maximize tax refunds, and track their success along the way by providing them with critical methods and resources. Let us take these measures together and equip our young adults to embark on a path of financial prosperity.

1. *Calculate the amount they want to save:* The idea is that emergency funds should cover at least half a year's worth of expenses. So, to get the figure they want to save, they should calculate or figure out what their expenses for six months will look like and how much they will cost. To be on the safe side, if possible, I also recommend an additional 10% security buffer.

2. *Set a monthly savings goal:* Saving will become easier if they have an idea of what their expenses for six months will look like. Divide the money they want to save into months and then, considering the amount they earn each month, they can decide on an amount to save each month.

Advise them to make savings through an automatic bank transfer. Let them send a percentage of their salary to a savings account. If their employer offers that option, they might be able to divide their pay into several checking and savings accounts. This will help them meet their saving goals easily without touching their checking account.

3. Teach them to pile up the change: Now is the time they should start treating their change with respect and value. Some people do not value tiny amounts like, say, $1 or $5. They sometimes leave change behind or use it up because they feel it is not worth saving.

Give your child a task—let them keep their change in a jar each time they make a purchase and see how much it turns out to be by the end of the month. They might be shocked at how much they have in the jar. You must teach them to save automatically after purchases. In this way, they will have more money to save. There are saving-focused apps that link with your accounts to round up any amount when you purchase something. The extra amount is then automatically transferred to your savings account.

4. Save your tax refund: This is an opportunity they can only get once a year in the U.S., though this may not be a possibility in every country. They can direct their tax refund to their emergency fund if they are expecting one. They can also have less money withheld by adjusting their W-4 tax form, which would result in extra cash they can stash away to their emergency fund.

Advise your child to closely monitor their saving progress to know when to adjust it or make a change. There might be a need to increase their weekly or monthly savings, especially if they just withdrew from it.

Reaching the milestone of having six months' worth of expenses saved is not a call to stop saving, however, you can advise them to start another savings account, so they are not tempted to spend from it. It is also important to save for irregular things like vacations, clothing, etc. Many banks can help you do this by creating a sub-savings account for your different financial goals.

INVEST LIKE A PRO: THE COST-AVERAGE EFFECT

An important concept that you should know is the cost-average effect. I will help you to easily understand why this effect is a powerful tool for successfully building wealth with regular ETF investments.

The cost-average effect is the result of a savings plan. It smooths out the costs of buying a security on the stock exchange. You do not invest one-time amounts in individually selected securities, but instead, you regularly invest the same amount in the same security or a portfolio of securities.

It all sounds complicated. But it is not. The cost-average effect is most easily explained by a calculation example. For simplicity, I assume strong price fluctuations. Please keep in mind, that in the real world, smaller fluctuations occur on the stock exchange, so investors may receive several fractions of the individual shares.

Investor A buys shares of an ETF for $100 every month via an ETF savings plan. He receives the following shares:

SAVING & INVESTING

Month	Price per share	Monthly Investment	Purchased shares
Jan	$50.00	$100.00	2.0
Feb	$40.00	$100.00	2.5
Mar	$20.00	$100.00	5.0
Apr	$25.00	$100.00	4.0
May	$40.00	$100.00	2.5
Jun	$50.00	$100.00	2.0
	Ø $33.33	∑ $600.00	∑ 18.0

After the savings plan has run for 6 months, investor A has invested a total of $600 and received 18 shares in return. On average, each fund share cost $33.33.

Investor B decides to buy 3 shares every month. The price for the shares in this savings plan depends on the changing prices:

Month	Price per share	Monthly Investment	Purchased shares
Jan	$50.00	$150.00	3.0
Feb	$40.00	$120.00	3.0
Mar	$20.00	$60.00	3.0
Apr	$25.00	$75.00	3.0
May	$40.00	$120.00	3.0
Jun	$50.00	$150.00	3.0
	Ø $37.50	∑ $675.00	∑ 18.0

Investor B also has 18 shares in his securities account after 6 months. However, he has paid a total of $675 for the shares. The average price for the shares is $37.50.

If both investors choose an ETF savings plan, the cost-average impact demonstrates the advantage of a fixed savings amount over a fixed number of shares acquired each month.

When prices are low, and you invest a fixed amount you receive more shares, while fewer shares are purchased when prices rise. This creates the effect of a more favorable average price than when the saver buys a fixed number of shares each month.

However, some experts see more than just advantages in the cost average effect. The main criticism is that cost-averaging results in lower returns (in most cases) compared to a one-time investment, making it the inferior investment strategy.

This is correct.

However, you will use it for asset accumulation, and for this purpose it is best suited. In addition, it teaches your child (and you!) to invest in a disciplined way, because investment amounts and timing are clear from the start. Most likely you won't spend your money elsewhere.

RECAP

Teaching children about saving involves instilling the concept of delayed gratification, a critical financial discipline. Despite many adults struggling with saving, patience and encouragement can help children develop this vital habit. Statistics highlight the challenge, with only 16% of Americans saving more than 15% of their income.

Emergency funds play a crucial role in handling unexpected expenses, preventing reliance on credit cards or loans. Children should learn to distinguish between real emergencies and non-urgent needs, emphasizing the importance of financial buffers.

Guidelines suggest saving at least 10-15% of income and maintaining an emergency fund covering three to six months of expenses. Accessible, high-yield savings accounts are recommended for these funds.

Investing early introduces children to the power of compound interest, significantly boosting long-term financial growth. Practical steps, like using familiar companies for investments, make the process engaging and educational.

For younger children, saving goals can be fun and tangible, using tools like piggy banks and wish lists to prioritize and save for desired items. Preteens should learn to differentiate between needs and wants, understand basic financial management, and set realistic saving goals. These lessons lay a strong foundation for financial literacy and future independence.

SPENDING
& DEBT

> *Debt is a form of enslavement to past events. You can't live well in the present time and plan for the future unless you learn how to break free of paying for the past.*
>
> – Tsh Oxenreider

For children, money can sometimes feel like it falls from the sky. That's why it's your job as their parent to educate them on how it's earned.

My wife and I came across extremely valuable research on the matter, which suggests an approach that is like what professionals in the field of formative brain science can be used by sponsors and advertisers, pediatricians, therapists, and instructors.

Here are a couple of essentials that will assist you with showing your children how to spend mindfully.

Mirror Your Child's Language

Younger kids might believe in Santa Claus, beasts under their bed, the power of Superman, and speaking dogs like the ones from PAW Patrol. The line between dream and truth is foggy for most young children. They regularly have dreams they swear truly occurred. Enchanted reasoning is a lifestyle for children, and along these lines, attempting to teach them solid habits like managing cash and saving can be a genuine challenge.

Enter your child's reality by adopting the thought process of children while discussing spending and saving in words they can comprehend. Discuss with your child about money and observe the words they use when looking at spending and saving. When the time comes to check what your child knows through a cash exercise, use their own words and expressions about money. Mirroring language helps your message resonate with your children—and it shows you listen when they talk.

Model the Right Behavior

Children watch you and tend to model after you, even when it comes to the simplest of things. Spending is not an exception. When it comes to spending there is an abundance of lessons to give your children. All you need to do is be observant and listen to them.

- *Every money transaction you make online and offline* is a learning opportunity for them. Let them see you do these transactions and, if they are curious, they might ask a question or two. Usually, their questions will expose what they know or do not know.
- *At the mall,* they can learn about spending. When you use your card, tell them it is the money you put in there. Work with a budget and stick to it, let them help you make choices, and every time you pick up something and return it to the shelf let them know why you made the choice. Let them see the need for cost and value. One of the best ways to teach children is by letting them see. They're more likely to remember what they see or have practiced.
- *At the grocery store*: Take them shopping for the house. Let them help you make the shopping list. Let them be part of the shopping process, comparing prices and sticking to what the house needs. You can pay with cash if you get the chance. This drives home the point that once you spend money, it is gone. They can put their knowledge of bills and denominations into practice.

- *A pharmacy* is also a place where they can learn and practice their spending lessons. Use cash if you can so that they can be familiar with cash as well.
- *Restaurants*: When you go out to eat, make the most of the opportunity and add to your children's spending knowledge and experience.
- *Game*: Using games to teach children about money goes back a few generations. Technology has made it easier now. Use board games as a teaching medium. Playing monopoly has proved effective for many parents and is a lot of fun! Technology has even made it possible for us to have Monopoly apps on our smartphones or tablets.

Let Them Live and Learn

It took some time for my parents to trust me with spending money—my mom especially. Not really because she knew for sure that I was going to make mistakes, or that it was going to be hard on me, but because I think she was not that quick in accepting that one of her babies was fast-growing and becoming exposed to life and reality, and so should be as prepared as possible for the future. She had a way of thinking I was not grown-up enough to handle certain responsibilities, which I know now I should have been handling.

Well, I later found out that a lot of parents are like that. They are either scared their children will make mistakes when they get handed over certain responsibilities, or they think their children are not grown enough to handle financial responsibilities. They instead allow them to be dependent on them for everything.

Do not raise your children with fear. Do not wait until it looks obvious or likely that they can take care of certain financial responsibilities before you give them those responsibilities. Give them responsibilities children at their age should be handling, expect them to make few mistakes, and then teach them how to handle money better. They learn better on the field.

Let me provide you with a practical example to illustrate the importance of allowing children to live and learn when it comes to financial responsibilities:

Imagine you have a 12-year-old child named Alexa. Alexa has shown interest in earning her own money and taking on financial responsibilities. Instead of dismissing her enthusiasm or being overly cautious, you decide to embrace this opportunity to teach her valuable lessons about money management.

You sit down with Alexa and discuss her desire to earn money. Together, you come up with a plan for her to take on certain responsibilities around the house, such as doing extra chores, mowing the lawn, or even babysitting. These tasks will not only contribute to the household but also allow Alexa to earn an income.

You explain to Alexa that with this newfound income, she will be responsible for managing some of her own finances. You provide guidance on the importance of budgeting and differentiating between needs and wants. You encourage her to allocate a portion of her earnings for savings, some for spending on personal interests, and perhaps even a small portion for charitable giving.

As Alexa starts receiving her earnings, you must resist the urge to micromanage her choices. Instead, you support and observe her decision-making process. For instance, Alexa may initially spend her money on small treats, which she later realizes do not provide long-term satisfaction. This experience becomes a teachable moment, where you discuss the concept of delayed gratification and the value of saving for bigger goals.

Over time, Alexa begins to understand the importance of financial discipline. She starts setting her own savings goals, such as saving for a bicycle or a special event with friends. As she encounters occasional financial setbacks or makes less-than-optimal choices, you can offer guidance and help her understand the consequences of her decisions.

Through this hands-on approach, Alexa learns the true value of money, develops essential financial skills, and gains confidence in managing her own finances. By allowing her to make mistakes and providing support along the way, you empower her to become a financially responsible individual who is perfectly equipped to handle future financial challenges.

Remember, the key is to strike a balance between granting responsibilities and offering guidance, and creating an environment where children can learn, grow, and become financially independent individuals.

From Impulse to Intention: Guiding Children Towards Financial Responsibility

I taught a friend an effortless way to help her son to become more responsible with spending and less careless with his things.

She complained that her son did not know how to manage money or anything bought with money. He always expected her to have the money to provide for everything and so he used things roughly without a thought about the consequences. She had tried denying him the things he asked for, but it only put a strain on their relationship. He thought she was just being mean. She just could not bear that as a single mom, so she decided it was better to save the relationship at the cost of financial literacy.

I understood the tricky situation she was in, so I thought: "What if you let the boy know the true cost of things?"

Children do not know the true cost of things unless they are faced with it. I am not just talking about price tags here. I mean they do not necessarily know what it costs to get some of the things they demand. The shoes you buy for $1,000 when you only have $1,500 in your bank account cost more in terms of the overall impact on your lifestyle than the shoes you buy for $1,000 when you have $3,000 to spend. Children do not always know this. They just look at you as a provider and are not always concerned about how you do it.

My friend and I came up with a plan to let her son learn how much things cost by bringing him into the budgeting process and then handing him over the responsibility of buying some of the things needed at home. She made the whole budgeting process transparent and easy for him to understand, but she secretly and deliberately under-budgeted for some things, whilst being fully aware of their true cost.

Then came the last step of the plan: She gave her son cash to go buy basic things like toiletries, some school materials for his younger siblings, a couple of other things, and the video gamepad he wanted to replace. Remember that, because she had under-budgeted, he was not given enough cash to buy all the things needed, which he did not know.

I was hoping he would make the right decision and he did. He ended up buying the most important and pressing things, and he left out his gamepad for later. Surprisingly, he was not that sad about not getting those things for himself because he, too, felt he made the right decisions. With time and exercises like that, the nagging desire to get everything right away reduced drastically, and he became more responsible with money and handling his things in general.

He learned an important lesson that day: the true cost of things. My friend doesn't regret teaching her son how to become financially literate and intelligent. Now she has taken it beyond the level of giving him buying responsibilities by giving him the responsibility of covering some expenses from his own pocket.

Let Your Child Have Purchasing Responsibilities

Children become more aware as they grow older, but they still need a little bit of help to face the reality completely. When you give them purchasing responsibilities, they start learning the true cost of things and how to arrange their budget to accommodate both wants and needs. There are a couple of spending responsibilities you could hand over to them, then just watch them and make suggestions on how they could manage their expenses to get all they need and want.

Give them responsibilities like buying most of their clothing and school supplies through their savings. They should also take responsibility for their snack money. Older teens should not depend on you for things like money to eat out with friends, go to the movies, and buy games. Let your kids handle these little expenses, once you are sure it's something their saving capacity can handle, and this will make them wise financially.

Handling little expenses will not be as difficult as you might think. Children can fund their wardrobe expenses from their recurring allowance. Shopping on sales-tax-free days (e.g., the Back-to-School Tax-Free Weekend, Veterans Day or Memorial Day Sales-Tax-Free Days) will also be helpful if you're in the United States. Longer-term expenses might include things like buying electronics, summer experiences, etc.

Teach them how to make and use budgets effectively. Depending on the amount of responsibility you give them, have them make their budgets to help them monitor their spending and purchases throughout the month or week. You can also introduce them to a budgeting tool to make things easier and faster for them.

Chances are they will make mistakes or get confused at times. They might have issues, like their spending not aligning with their budget. When such problems arise, do not just rush to solve them. Help them figure out or identify the root of the problem and only suggest ways they can solve it when you have first heard them out.

Make a connection between financial responsibility and personal finance

Training children is a difficult and serious task, especially when it has to do with money. But if they still come to you for money, you must give them the right response. Understand that your child's spending behavior (especially from ages 13 to 17) is mostly fueled by their need for independence. Just pause and think of the crazy things your children spend money on at this age, such as, limited edition sneakers, celebrity merchandise, cosplay costumes, designer accessories, or virtual in-game items. They might not even see it as unreasonable, even though it is.

When it comes to financial negotiations, parents and children frequently have opposing ideas and goals. You may emphasize financial responsibility, saving, and long-term planning, while your children, particularly teenagers, may prioritize their immediate desires, independence, and personal spending choices. This contrast in interests can lead to conflicts and disagreements during money-related conversations, creating a metaphorical "tug-of-war" situation where both of you try to pull the discussion in the preferred direction. Knowing this inevitable conflict helps you to lay foundation for their independence, rather than giving them the opportunity to turn their quest for independence into a way of challenging your authority and control. Children are more likely to argue with you as teenagers than they would have at any other stage of their life. (I am deliberately lumping all teenagers together here.)

This tug-of-war must be avoided before it spills into other parts of your relationship and life. To win the war, you must find a way to make connections between financial responsibility and personal independence. You must skillfully shift the direction of such conversations.

In her journal *More than Money*, Anne Ellinger, a nonprofit peer education networker, demonstrated how to shift the course of such a discussion with your children to a higher level.[45]

As a result, when I say "no" to something my son wants to buy or do, I have coached him to ask me: "What will help?" I then think aloud and share my thought process with him: "I want you to learn how to budget and save for the things you desire. This is a life skill that many individuals lack, as well as the ability to communicate effectively. So, I am asking you to reevaluate the need of spending money on this (trip, item, etc.). To be honest, I'd be prepared to spend half the price if you wanted something that might help you improve as a person. But if you don't put the money to good use, I'll expect you to pay me back." Even if he's angry with me, he can see that I'm not just imposing my will on him.

With this technique, your child will see that you care about what they are saying and that you are willing to help them, but then you want to teach them something better. This is something different from the tug-of-war that would normally ensue. This conflict makes them feel like you are a threat to their independence, and like you are supervising their every move. Once this happens, it will be difficult for them to listen to any other thing you have to say.

You can see here that the conversation shifts the tone from a war of wills to that of a collaboration in problem-solving, which is what I prefer in every situation. Your children will also learn the power of problem-solving and good judgment. You must start implementing and practicing this technique on your kids now. You can even personalize it a bit to suit your context. Add questions like: How will this trip, action, or choice affect your budget, savings account, plans, and checking account?

The lesson of making connections between choices and their financial impact is so important to the financial development of your children. It will change the way they spend, save, and do everything else. There is no better time to teach them this than when they have something at stake. And as previously shown, this is often the case with teenagers.

Make them understand the truth that they will always experience a shortage of funds and resources and their needs will often outweigh their resources no matter who they are and how rich they are. You must teach them these things with every slightest opportunity you get.

If your child brings up a need or opportunity after you have made your financial plan as a family, the first thing to do should not be to check whether or not you can afford the expense. That is not particularly important at this point. The first thing to do is to check in with your children and make sure they can evaluate and look at that opportunity considering the ongoing financial plan of the family.

You should ask questions like: Is there a way for you to earn some extra cash to take care of this new expense whilst keeping the budget balanced?

Teach your child this wisdom with every opportunity you get. If your child walks up to you and says they want to go on a backpacking trip or any kind of fun trip or activity, ask them questions like: How can you show me that you have the sound judgment and discipline to make this a good financial decision as well as a fun choice?

Their plan at that point may not have a lot to do with money, but it is important to ask such questions to help them make the connection early enough. Questions like the following will also do a lot of good:

- Are they using their own money for entrance fees, food, travel expenses, and equipment?
- Is that how they want to spend their money?
- What will they have left to save later if they do this now?

SPENDING & DEBT

Credit cards and the debt problem

There is never an end to spending issues. The problem as you get older is always about differentiating between wants and needs. But at the ages of 18 to 21, young adults might even have a bigger problem: the debt problem. They have gotten to an age where they can freely use credit cards, and credit card companies will already be lurking around them with different offers. But please refer to the discussion on the challenges and pitfalls of accumulating college debt.

You must treat the lesson on credit cards with significant importance, since, if not, your children could easily find themselves in debt. With a new credit card comes the feeling of abundance and freedom to spend as much as you want. But the more you spend, the greater debt you go into. It feels like you have free money, but your children must understand that a credit card is nothing more than a form of loan.

They are simply using the card issuer's money, with a limit placed on it. Now, this comes with a cost—they must pay interest for using another person's money. Let them know it is just like borrowing money from a friend. The balance they see in their credit card statement is not their money, it is just a possible amount of money they can borrow now. And if they do not repay it when they should, they will have to pay interest.

When you think you are getting free money, you may be eager to take more. This is exactly what some young adults do when they just start using credit cards.

Use credit calculators to show your children how much interest they can accrue by not paying back loans or by consistently carrying a balance (you can find a lot of those on the internet).

Explain the consequences of carrying a large balance so they can avoid it at all costs.

Debt is an integral part of financial literacy. But you do not have to wait for your children to get into debt before you start teaching them about it. You must be careful on how to teach this concept. Do not go into simplifying it as: "Debt is bad and evil," to save them from debt. Instead, teach them the difference between good and bad debt. Remember, be as realistic as possible at this stage as the stakes are higher. They are moving from a demo account to a live account now.

> *Good debt is when you borrow money to buy an asset.*
> *Bad debt is when you borrow money to buy a liability.*
>
> *– Andrea Stephenson*

Constructive Debt

Constructive debt is key to building wealth. It is any debt used to increase your wealth, which includes things like education, mortgages, etc. Mortgages are part of constructive debts because they can be a route to becoming a homeowner. And, of course, homeownership does not just provide shelter. Real estate can be a vital part of amassing personal wealth.

Money used to advance education can shorten the process to personal wealth because education can expose you to opportunities and increase your earning potential.

Business loans to start or scale a business are also an example of constructive debt. This kind of debt can be an advantage in building personal wealth as long as the debt is handled well.

Overall, constructive debt is important for your children's finances. The key is being able to pay it back and control it instead of letting it control you.

Bad Debt

Then there is bad debt, which is the exact opposite of constructive debt. Going into debt to fund your lifestyle is an example of bad debt. If you do not teach your children to avoid bad debt, they will risk falling into bad debt and struggling financially for the rest of their lives. One bad debt could drain all of one's assets, no matter how big it is.

There are four major but simple ways to identify or spot bad debt which you should teach your children:

1. *Bad debt is not used to build assets or wealth*. This is money borrowed for consumption purposes, to purchase goods and services that do not help in building your overall wealth or asset portfolio.

2. *High repayment interests*. Teach your children to run away from any debt that comes with a high repayment interest. If they do not, they might spend years paying back debts instead of building their wealth.

3. *If the ratio of debt versus interest fees is disproportionate*, then it is awfully bad debt. Teach them not to get into any debt that will dry them up every month. If it is not a debt they can comfortably pay back every month, then it is bad debt. For example, imagine you have a credit card with a $5,000 balance and an annual interest rate of 20%. You're making minimum payments each month, but due to the high interest rate, the majority of your payment goes

towards covering the interest fees rather than reducing the principal debt.

4. *If the interest on debt is not tax-deductible*, then it may be bad debt. However, one must be careful here, because often only interest from owner-occupied real estate is tax-deductible for private individuals.

If your children watch out for these signs, they should be on a smooth road to freedom from bad debt. You must watch out for them because they do not always think of the consequences of their actions. They might borrow money for just about anything and end up struggling.

Sometimes they will borrow money knowing that mom and dad are there to help in the very worst-case scenario. When they rely on you to clear their debt, do not just eagerly come to their rescue. Do not clear their debts, and instead teach them how everything has consequences and they should be ready to take responsibility for their actions.

They should take responsibility for any expense they incur without your knowledge or approval.

Building a healthy credit score

A lot of parents fear talking to their children about credit cards. I understand their fear. Many people have gone bankrupt and are in heavy debt because of credit card companies. Some parents are even struggling right now due to the way they used their credit cards. However, credit cards are important to teach children some important lessons like building an excellent credit score.

A credit score is a number between 300-850 that shows a consumer's creditworthiness. A credit score is evaluated through a person's credit history. Owning and using a credit card is one of the fastest ways to build a healthy credit score. Children might not know the essence of building a credit score at that age. A good credit score is particularly important in the real world which they just started experiencing; in fact, it is a necessary survival tool. Without a good credit score, for example, you might end up not getting loans to build your wealth.

Remember you should have taught them about good loans and bad loans by now. So, they know how important a loan can be in building wealth and assets. Even if they can get loans, it might be with higher interest rates. You might pay higher interest for things like car loans and mortgages. A good credit score is often one of the requirements required by some landlords to rent out their apartments.

Let your children know that eyes are on them, watching how they make use of their credit cards. Maybe this will make them make wiser decisions.

Fact: A single past due payment can result in a 90-to-110-point decrease for a person with a credit score of 780(+).

Credit card issuers report your credit card activities to the credit bureau every month. A credit bureau is a data collection agency that collects account information from various creditors and sends it to a consumer reporting agency. The bureau will know how much you owe and how faithful you have been in paying off your debts. This report determines how credit-worthy you are.

Credit scores do not just appear from nowhere. Two major things determine someone's credit score:

- The first one is payment history. This accounts for 35% of one's FICO credit score.* Missing the originally scheduled day of payment will harm your account; it brings down your credit score, whereas paying responsibly when payments are due will increase your credit score.
- Another major factor that determines what your credit score looks like is credit utilization. They must be careful with how they use their credit cards because it has a direct reflection on their credit score. Simply having a credit balance does not mean you should use it carelessly. Using more than 50% of the credit and carrying a balance each month will harm their credit score, while using less than 30% of the credit will increase their credit score.

---

* FICO Scores, developed by Fair Isaac Corporation, are the most widely used credit scores. 90% of the top lenders use FICO Scores to make credit-related decisions. The score estimates the level of future credit risk, or how likely it is that a loan gets repaid. Therefore, this information is compared to data patterns of past credit reports. The scores are based solely on data maintained by the credit bureaus Experian, Equifax, and TransUnion.

5 Things impacting your Credit Score

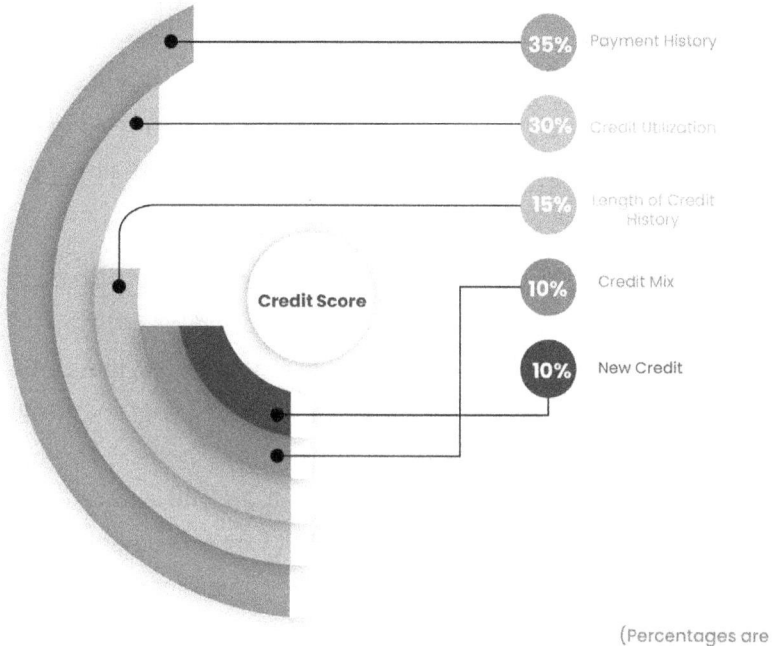

- 35% Payment History
- 30% Credit Utilization
- 15% Length of Credit History
- 10% Credit Mix
- 10% New Credit

Credit Score

(Percentages are based on FICO score. Scores range between 300 and 850.)

A young adult must cultivate the right credit habits to maintain a good credit score. How long you have used your credit card, the types of credit cards you use, and how recently you applied for a credit card all determine what your credit score will look like. Your children must know this, too.

A Guide to Credit Cards for Children

When your child gets their own bank account, the question of debit and credit cards naturally comes up. And this conversation, which every parent must have with their children, must convey the extent of the responsibility of owning a debit or credit card. The conversation does not have to be technical, but it must imprint upon them the importance of it.

Let us talk about credit cards some more: Preteens and teens get excited at the thought of owning one, but their excitement can come from the wrong reasons. Most likely, they love the power of being able to buy anything they want or need without asking for their parent's permission. Teach them early so that the reality sinks in before they get old enough to own one.

Teenagers ought to understand that credit cards can be an incredible tool when they are used effectively. They need to understand the risks associated with owning a credit card, for instance, the fact that credit card charges can ruin your financial stability. If you or your spouse do not know enough about credit cards to explain the risks to your children, take the time to first educate yourself, and think about when the correct time is for them to own one. Start with fundamental cash concepts first. Allow your children to acquire some experience going through cash they procure as a reward or tackling chores. You may even allow them to borrow cash from you a couple of times to show them how credit works.

What your children should know about using credit cards

When the time comes, here are the things your children should be aware of:

Mistakes will follow you for a long time

Credit card mistakes are common, and they can be hard to fix. Help your child imagine the difficulty that could come from credit mistakes. For instance, when they are looking for work, a company may check your child's credit report and choose to instead employ somebody with a spotless financial record. Or when your child tries to rent or buy a property, the property manager may turn them down due to bad credit card debt. They may be unable to get an advance on a car on account of past credit issues.

When your child has a credit card, check in with them sometimes to know how things are going and help respond to any questions they have. Ensure you are providing the right answers and guiding them toward solid goals. It is an empowering responsibility, but one for which they should be ready.

It is not your cash, and it is not free

Children frequently grow up thinking their parents' credit cards are simple sorcery. You need to let them understand that credit cards need to be repaid, and the longer it takes, the more interest they are accruing. The main thing to teach them is that a credit card only allows them to use another person's cash. The bank consents to allow a cardholder to acquire a specific amount of cash, again and again, as long it is reimbursed. The balance can be reimbursed right away or over time, but your children should realize that the more time it takes to repay the balance, the more the interest payments will add up and they should know how and when interest is charged.

Do not skip installment payments

Some parents have limitless tolerance with their children, who regularly take it for granted. Yet, children should discover that not everybody will be as patient, particularly not with regards to cash and late credit card payment fees.

Explain to your children that, while the credit loaner will not thump on the entryway for a missed installment (though if it becomes too high, they might), they will charge fees. They will also call, send letters, and may eventually choose to sue for a neglected credit balance, regardless of the sum. Worse even, credit card companies report late installments to the credit authorities, which will harm one's odds of getting another credit card in the future. If you have co-signed on a credit card application for your children, ensure they understand that you are also at risk for their credit errors.

Have a one mistake limit—one missed installment, one over-the-limit expense—and afterward, close the account until they are prepared to be more responsible.

Do not depend on your credit card

Since credit and debit cards look practically indistinguishable, your child may have grown up thinking you have used your credit card for every one of your purchases. Clarify that a credit card is not intended for staples like food and gas. This behavior can lead to accumulating interest charges, overspending, and credit card debt. To encourage responsible financial habits, it is important to teach children budgeting, saving, and the distinction between needs and wants. Emphasizing the appropriate use of a credit card for essential and important payments can help children develop a better understanding of managing their finances.

Show your children that their credit card only provides the money they have and that it is not to be utilized for unimportant or unessential things.

There is a limit to what you can buy

Credit card companies enforce a credit limit—a maximum balance the cardholder can use. Caution your children against piling up enormous debt since that will hold them back from having the option to use their credit card when something significant comes up. Keeping a low balance on their card also means it is simpler to pay off and helps improve their credit score.

Do not let anyone or anything impact buying decisions

This pressure usually comes from friends, social media, television, and so on. Credit card usage should not be a result of peer pressure or online adverts. Be certain your child understands the effects of advertising. Teach them to settle on sound spending choices by avoiding hasty purchases. Have discussions with them about how their peers impact their decisions, and how they can be aware of that. Ultimately, your children are responsible for the credit card bill, not their friends, and not television or web advertisers.

Use or get a credit card only when you are sure that you can manage it

Using credit cards as payment when they cannot afford to pay them back prompts issues like missed installments, late expenses, higher interest, and an awful credit score. Your children must understand their affordability in the short term before using their credit card. If you are not going to protect your children from their credit card mishaps, let them know from the start and stick to your guns. Many children are bound to be more responsible with their money when they know their parents will not step in to fix their slip-ups.

Card security

In this tech world, children are turning into digital natives at younger ages than ever before. Consequently, it is fundamental to give your kid guidance to ensure their financial security online both now and later.

Here are a few ways to show your children financial safety on the web, for instance:

As hacking grows more sophisticated, more credit card details are being stolen every year due to web purchases and internet use. It is essential to establish rules for using credit cards securely online so children understand that they should be cautious about where they input their credit card information. Assist children with understanding when a site appears to be protected and like an authentic business, and when it appears to be a trick. Outline what could happen to them if that they give their card information to a fraudulent website.

Keeping away from game and application purchases

It can be enticing for small children to want to buy games on the internet. Particularly dangerous are the in-application buys that many game designers embed into their games to encourage children to spend more. (You can read more about this in the section about gaming traps.)

As a parent, you must ensure that your child understands that they are spending actual cash and not game money. A few children probably will not have the experience or practical insight to be able to use a credit card safely online. To secure your card data, set rules about spending money on the internet. Those rules could be that they have a spending limit they are allowed that is monitored intently. You can also set up two-factor authentications.

Other than cards, there are different options to assist children with spending money online safely, for example, virtual credit cards, or through other cashless applications.

Information safety

Inexperienced children need to understand that they should be careful about safeguarding sensitive information when dealing with cash on the web or talking to other people. Should they not practice sound judgment in these matters, they might be putting you and your family in danger of data fraud. This also applies to information they post on social media, so help them understand the need to safeguard sensitive information when posting on social media because this is one of the ways fraudsters get answers to personal questions, such as date of birth, where you live, mother's birth name, etc.

Password security

Showing your children how to create secure passwords is the first step in keeping information secure. Ensure that they understand they should not pick a password that's too obvious, for example, their birthdate or pet name.

It is also useful to urge them to create longer passwords with more special characters as an extra layer of safety. There are also apps, like Keeper, that can help them to generate and store complex passwords. It is equally important to have complex usernames. Go through password and username "best practices" with your child (it's easy to find these resources online).

Social media security

As more children start utilizing web-based media at younger ages, it is imperative to have genuine discussions with your children about how they should be careful of what they post online. For instance, ensure your children know not to post details of a trip while they're away from home, as that may welcome burglars into your home.

With a little presence of mind and awareness, parents can help show their children how to monitor the financial security of their families. These lessons will stay with your children forever and help them as they grow into responsible adults.

PRACTICE BUDGETING FOR THE FUTURE

As your children enter their teenage years, the future becomes more tangible and relevant. It's important for them to move beyond vague and unrealistic ideas and develop a clearer, more realistic vision of what they want their future to look like. While the pursuit of independence may sometimes distract them from this awareness, this stage presents a valuable opportunity to expand their horizons and consider the financial implications of their life choices.

Practical Budgeting Exercises

I recommend you give your children practical lifestyle budgeting habits. This is quite easy to do, and it is a powerful revelation, too.

You can go about it like this:

1. Make a big list of professions or jobs and make your children choose a job they want to actively earn money from by the age of 25. Do not criticize or judge any of their choices.
2. Next, have them search the web for the average entry-level income for that choice. On the Internet, they will easily find information on job finder sites.
3. Have them note down that income on a piece of paper (call it a balance sheet).
4. Now, ask them to make some lifestyle choices. To do this, you must provide them with a sample budget. The numbers on your sample budget should reflect the average national figures for your local area.

Once your children have made their selection, have them fill this into the Budget Worksheet.

Joline Godfrey, in her book *Raising Financially Fit Kids,* describes the effect of the budget lifestyle exercise.

According to her, the idea of "entry-level" is strange to children, as they have been taught that attaining celebrity status and fortune is as easy as snapping your fingers. At least, this is what they might have learned from various reality TV shows. Hence, they may believe they can get immediate gratification on anything, just like their TV show stars and heroes. This is the moment to instill a sense of truth in your children regarding lifestyle choices and independence. To let them know that reality is different from what they see on TV.

Budgeting Habits: A Story

During my research, I found two situations that I would like to present here. These show that there are just as many individual reactions and solutions as there are children. (I'm sorry that these examples are very gender biased, but it was important to me to bring real examples.)

A young lady who has always wanted to be a model and live a luxurious lifestyle realized that entry-level models start earning just $4,000 per year. She soon dropped her unrealistic ideas and became practical when she saw that the lifestyle she had chosen required her to own a house and drive an SUV, which are expensive items. She started thinking along the lines of what she must do better to achieve her dream. Finally, she listed out several options like taking another job, cutting down on her expenses, and saving.

A young man who chose to pursue basketball as a career was stunned to see that entry-level salaries for NBA rookies averaged about $73,000 (for WNBA rookies this is only $30,000—can you spell Title IX?) and that very few players made as much as the megastars. He did not give up his dream but broadened his vision to consider owning a team, managing a team, being a coach, or being an agent. As he looked at what it would take to get where he wanted to go, he was able to make a connection between his career timeline and the lifestyle choices he would need to make, such as, sacrificing personal expenses, devoting long hours to studying, and balancing work-life commitments.

Lifestyle budget tests always have this kind of revelation effect on people. It is a great way of bringing children back to the reality of things. The essence of this is not to scare them away from dreaming big. It just makes them financially conscious of the dreams and targets they want to realize in the future.

HOW WE CAN HELP OUR CHILDREN BUILD A GOOD CREDIT SCORE FROM AN EARLY AGE THROUGH CREDIT CARDS

If the only way you can build an emergency fund is to pay the minimum due on your credit card, that is what you need to do.

– Suze Orman

Become an Authorized User

At 18, your children can own an individual credit card. Age is not a factor when it comes to determining credit scores, but it surely has an indirect effect or influence on it. At 18, for example, your children will have a thin credit file. This of course does not add anything to their credit score. To build their credit, they can become an authorized user on another person's credit card. Becoming an authorized user means they will enjoy the benefits of an older account, especially if it has had a good record over the years.

You could advise your children to start building their credit with your card if you have maintained a good record over the years. There is no disadvantage in doing this. You will be responsible for helping in the credit building process; they do not even have to be using the card to be recognized as an authorized user. But before you make your children an authorized user of your card, make sure the card company also reports the activities of that authorized user to the three major card bureaus, as some of them don't. Your child's credit report will be generated from this report.

A Credit Builder Loan

One of the ways to help your children build their credit record is to advise them to take out a credit builder loan. They can do this through the help of credit unions and community banks. Here is how credit loans work; unlike other types of loans, credit loans stay in a savings account, and you cannot access them until the end of the loan term.

You must make on-time payments towards the loan. This is nice because the bank or whatever institution they borrowed from will report this activity to the credit bureaus. And this will have an exceptionally good effect on their credit score because at the end of the loan term it will have improved, as they have fulfilled the contractual obligations. This saves them money in the future because a good credit score determines (among other factors) the interest to be paid. The logic behind this is quite simple: Those who have paid off debts in the past will most likely do so in the future. Accordingly, interest rates are lower (the risk premium decreases), as the probability that debts will be settled by the debtor increases.

Secured or No Deposit Credit Card

This is yet another option for building a credit score. Secured cards are the best option for young adults. It requires you to have a deposit of about $200 – $2000 which will serve as your line of credit. It is generally best they use secured credit cards or credit cards that do not require a security deposit.

Secured cards are important and useful because if you are unable to pay the balance when it is due, the company will take the money automatically from your deposit. So, you will always pay for the loan somehow, either by paying it back on time or by the company taking their money themselves from your deposit. If you can pay back the whole loan on time, you will get your deposit back.

You will need a certain amount of income to qualify for a secured credit card. Before applying for one, also make sure that it reports to at least one credit bureau. Always advise your children to pay off their full balance on time at the end of every month. A secured credit card is ideal for your children for a start. With it, they can build their credit report, and later go for a traditional unsecured credit card. Note, however, that traditional unsecured cards still require a steady income from a full-time job.

RECAP

Debt ties you to the past, making it difficult to enjoy the present or plan for the future. Teaching children about money is essential, as they often see it as unlimited. Use their language to explain financial concepts and model good habits by involving them in everyday transactions like shopping and budgeting. This helps them grasp the true cost of things.

Assign age-appropriate financial responsibilities to children. Allow them to make mistakes and learn from them. Use practical budgeting exercises to illustrate the financial impact of their choices, teaching them to differentiate between needs and wants.

Clarify the concept of debt, distinguishing between constructive debt (such as education or a mortgage) that builds wealth and bad debt that drains resources. Explain that credit cards are loans requiring repayment with interest. Emphasize the importance of building a good credit score through responsible credit management.

By guiding children through real-life financial experiences and instilling responsible financial practices, you prepare them to handle their future finances with confidence and wisdom.

GIVING BACK & ENTREPRENEURSHIP

Children enjoy gifts. As parents, it is our responsibility to teach them that it is not enough to receive. We should also give back, no matter how little.

You could use birthdays to teach them about this. Do something different. Instead of just receiving gifts, let them give out proceeds from their party to, for instance, a charity or someone in need.

Let your children see that they can be of assistance, and how. Show them that money can also be shared with people who are in need. Teach by example. Let them participate in your charity work, so they can learn some of this from your actions.

> *Before you speak, listen. Before you write, think. Before you spend, earn. Before you invest, investigate. Before you criticize, wait. Before you pray, forgive. Before you quit, try. Before you retire, save. Before you die, give.*
>
> – William A. Ward

Giving is an important part of financial literacy. Philanthropy is often believed to be something reserved for adults or very wealthy people. That is wrong. A person is never financially intelligent if they have not yet started giving back to society. There are a lot of things your children can learn by giving. For example, people who are taught giving from their childhood will learn that money will never be more valuable than family, society, or human beings generally, and that will affect the way they relate to others when it has to do with money. What I do regularly with my daughter, for example, is a toy collection campaign. We collect some of her old and new toys and donate them. In doing so, she learns how important it is to give back to others. My daughter experiences the joy of sharing and learns that money is not the most important thing in life, which helps her to develop empathy and a sense of social responsibility at a young age. I am certain that this early experience of giving will shape her perspective on money and that she has gained a lifelong understanding of philanthropy.

In looking to earn money, some people have forgotten and disregarded other values that should be held onto dearly. You do not want to raise children like that (I hope, at least, that we share the same values on this point). You do not have to be a millionaire to give, and neither do your children. You must teach them to give at every stage of their development.

HOW DO YOU TEACH THEM TO GIVE AT DIFFERENT AGES?

1. Talking about the needs in your community with your children will make them interested in looking for ways to help. Children normally look for the right opportunity to become heroes between 9 and 12 years old, because it boosts their self-confidence. All you must do is channel that desire properly. You might be able to encourage your children to make donations or partake in community service without them needing to be forced into it.
2. Do not force your children into community groups they do not wish to join. Allow them to choose the group they want to be in if there is nothing wrong with it.
3. Have a family giving ritual. You must lead by example: Having a family giving ritual will encourage and motivate your children to give. They will see it as a responsibility.

One of the rituals I have is to always give to charities on my birthday. I give in other situations too, but it is a ritual for me on birthdays. I give to foster homes, hospitals, etc. It does not have to be much, but I give as much as I can. You can choose Christmas, Easter, or any other memorable day for your family. Make it important and a mandatory tradition.

4. Encourage them to set out money to give back and add it to their budget. Let giving not be just an afterthought for them. It should be planned from the beginning of the year or every month. As I said, it does not have to be an outrageous amount. Let them give what they can. The most important thing is building the culture in them.

Young adults, however, should be giving more if they are earning more from part-time jobs or full-time jobs. They should be encouraged because, sometimes, responsibilities might be such that they consider reducing the amount they are used to giving. Encourage them, not under pressure, to adjust their budgets and find a way to give back.

SAFEGUARDING THE NEXT GENERATION THROUGH FINANCIAL LITERACY

Teenagers are extremely sensitive due to the many changes they go through, like hormonal shifts and social pressures. This makes them more emotional and self-conscious (even today, I already have respect for it when my daughter reaches that age). It puts how much your children have learned from you over the years to the test. If parents can provide steady support and understanding during this stage, they will find it easier to maintain a significant role in their children's lives. If you lose control, however, it might be difficult to get back to playing an important role in your child's life.

Most parents are usually scared for their children from the age of 13 onwards until they become responsible adults. Here, your child or children are seeking independence and are keen to express their personalities. They will soon become independent in every aspect and begin to experience the world in different ways. You cannot afford to let them leave the nest and get into real-life situations with only sugarcoated ideas and principles.

You know there is more to some of the things you have taught them already. There is more to being rich than not spending carelessly on everything you want. Children are often very dreamy (not realistic) before they get to experience real life for themselves.

Demo and Live Financial Environments

Let me put this into perspective for you. For example, when you start learning to trade on forex (when trading forex, two currencies are traded against each other; the purchase of one currency results in the simultaneous sale of the other), at some point after learning some basics, your teacher or coach opens a demo account for you to practice what you have learned. In that demo environment, people place successful trades and show that they have understood all they have been taught, then they open a live trading forex account to trade on. The experience when someone migrates from a demo account to a real live account is very often disappointing and discouraging. People think they have learned well, so they go and confidently place big trades, and many times they lose all their money.

You'll notice that a demo account and a real-life account are not the same, even though they look the same. You can see that the learning process is not complete yet, and there are things you still must learn to be able to survive in a real-life account.

Many teenagers in this age range are like the forex traders that think they have learned enough to go live life successfully. They begin to decide for themselves the way they want to live their life, what they want to do, and the friends they want to keep. All these things are signs of a person seeking independence and self-expression. Of course, they are not full adults yet so there is a limit to what they can do. They can keep making plans and taking small steps.

The few years left before your kid leaves the house should be used to start preparing them for the time they will finally set out on their own.

You must ask yourself how ready your children are for real life. How ready are they for the independence they will soon start fighting for? A lot of things will go wrong if they are not ready.

Raising a Debt-Aware Generation

According to a survey conducted by NBC News in April 2018, young adults aged 18 to 34 have a significant debt problem.[46]

Due to substantial debt, many young adults report delaying life steps. A third of young adults have delayed buying a home and/or saving for retirement, and approximately 15% have delayed marriage and/or having children.

According to a report released by the Federal Reserve Bank of New York, in 2019 alone the rate of credit card balances that were in 'serious delinquency'—meaning payments were at least 90 days overdue—for Americans between 18 and 29 years old hit an eight-year high.[47]

A Morning Consult poll from that same year states that 65% of millennials and 52% of Generation Z'ers who have credit card debt experience some or a lot of stress because of their debt.[48]

Another survey found that 35% feel guilty at least once a month because of their debt, while 20% reported feeling physically ill at least once a month.[49]

We must teach our teens more about money and debt if we want to raise the next generation to be responsible adults. When teens are swiping their credit cards for a fun purchase, it almost feels like 'free' money, so we must educate them that debt is not free at all.

The Importance of Ongoing Guidance

Many children are not prepared to manage real-life financial responsibilities. They might not understand how to budget, save, or avoid debt, leading some to overspend and accumulate bad debts they struggle to repay for years. This lack of preparedness underscores the importance of teaching your children financial literacy, not just for the well-being of your home but also for the stability of society as a whole.

As your children transition into young adulthood, it becomes clear how crucial this financial education is. Without proper guidance, many young adults find themselves financially overextended, struggling to manage their money effectively.

One of the reasons parents get overwhelmed when dealing with children aged 13 to 17 is that they expect them to be more responsible, financially and otherwise, and to need less guidance. However, this expectation can lead to frustration when teenagers exhibit behavior that seems less financially intelligent compared to when they were younger. For instance, they might impulsively spend money or disregard the budgeting habits they previously learned. This can be a difficult and complex period as teenagers strive to understand and connect with their true selves, develop genuine passions, and form personalized perspectives on life.

You were a child once, and you know how challenging this stage can be and how prone one is to making mistakes. Teenagers are not always focused on financial literacy at this point. Yes, they want a lot and there's a lot they want to do with their money, but many are more focused on self-expression rather than making wise financial decisions. They often seek money to prove their independence and show that they do not need their parents' financial protection. Sometimes, they may even spend recklessly just to demonstrate their autonomy.

Given this, parents must understand that raising a teenager can be challenging due to their desire for independence and self-expression. It's crucial to strike a balance between providing guidance and allowing them the freedom to make their own choices, learning from both successes and mistakes. This ongoing support and understanding are key to helping them develop into financially responsible adults.

Always Remember Instilling the Right Values

Always bear in mind that the teenage years are just a phase, and they will not last forever, but the way you handle this period of your child's life will affect your relationship and family dynamic in the future. The important thing is giving your child the right values so that, even when they reach their teenage years, they have the right value systems in place to guide them. Do not let their quest for independence deter you from the goal of raising them to become financially literate.

Instilling the right values includes teaching them the importance of budgeting, saving, and distinguishing between needs and wants. Encourage them to set financial goals, such as saving for a significant purchase or contributing to a college fund. Highlight the value of hard work and earning money through jobs or chores, and teach them about the consequences of debt and the importance of living within their means. As I said, teenagers at this stage are at risk of making bad financial decisions that might lead them into gradual debt in their lives. I think debt control is one of the most important things to teach your children. If you don't believe me, check out the statistics below[50]:

- A survey by Teenage Research Unlimited shows 11% of children aged 12 to 19 now have a credit card, while 10% also have access to their parent's credit card.

- The same survey reveals that teenagers spent an average of $103 per week, resulting in a total of $175 billion in 2003 alone.
- 85% of college students own at least one credit card, while 45% of them have an average debt of $3,000. In addition, 55% of them got their first credit card during their college years.
- Myvesta Organization found that it would take 39.5 years to pay off a $3,389 credit card debt with an interest of at least $9,098 if the payment is made following the monthly 18% interest rate.

ENTREPRENEURSHIP

> *People with low financial literacy standards are often unable to take their ideas and create assets out of them.*
>
> – Robert Kiyosaki

Children love trying new things. Often, they're smarter and more capable than adults think. For example, the children that made piggy banks with their dad were so excited that they told their friends at school, and they too wanted their piggy banks made from tins. The children chose to make more tin piggy banks and sell them to their friends. That was entrepreneurial, especially coming from 7-year-olds.

Encourage children to pursue entrepreneurial endeavors. Encouraging children to pursue entrepreneurial endeavors involves nurturing their creativity, problem-solving abilities, and business mindset at various stages of their development. For younger children, this can include setting up lemonade stands, creating handmade crafts to sell, or organizing small-scale community projects. As they grow older, even teenagers can explore online businesses, develop innovative apps or websites, or initiate social enterprises that address local or global challenges. The specific endeavors will vary based on your child's interests and capabilities, but the key is to provide guidance, resources, and mentorship to support their entrepreneurial journey at different ages and stages of their development.

When children learn to manage their own business, they are on their way to getting an A+ on their financial skills badge. Regardless of whether it is working a lemonade stand, mowing lawns, or even, in recent times, building a mobile application, there are a lot of ways in which children can become business visionaries*. It does not need to be a major achievement. Simply adopting an entrepreneurial attitude can help them develop fundamental skills and teach them significant financial lessons. There are incredible opportunities directly under your roof to encourage children to think about cash and business ventures.

By turning into business visionaries, children can learn about planning, saving, spending, and contributing.

"It makes you value cash more," said Thomas Henske, a certified financial planner with Lenox Advisors based in New York, who

---

* Today, a huge part of financial literacy is acquired by joining organizations like sports and art teams, student councils, etc. This is since it is always necessary to find ways to raise money and then this money should be managed for the organization.

created and now runs his company's savvy cash children program. "It's hard to make it. It's hard to keep it."[51]

When you open them up to things like conceptualizing and prototyping, they're likely to get it, which may help them with building determination by learning from their disappointments, as well as developing basic reasoning. Disappointment is important for the learning process. If they have a go at something and it does not work, rather than letting them quit, support them to continue.

You can ask, "What did you learn from that? How would you be able to improve things?"

Here are different ways you can motivate your children to become self-starters, whilst helping them to become savvy about cash:

1. Cultivating imagination

Children are often imaginative. They are not as compelled by history or limited by what they know. They are not terrified of being off base. Some children are not even scared of being told their ideas are insane, and they are not as afraid of disappointment as many adults are.

In this way, if your child has a good idea, be interested in it and help support it, regardless of whether it seems whacky.

2. Conceptualizing

Does your child need to figure out how to start earning cash? The main goal here is to ask them how they can get started. That is the place where conceptualizing comes in. Very few children might say, "I can rake the leaves," or "I can make the beds," only to have their parents respond with, "Goodness, could you construct a business around that?"

Financial planner Thomas Henske said he jumps at the chance to empower children to conceptualize by using mind maps. It can be as basic as getting a pen and paper or using an online tool.

For instance, his 15-year-old came to him for cash, since he had been unable to find a new job until after he turned 16. Henske turned it around and requested that he concoct a plan to procure it all alone. His children are currently building an application and site that connect children to neighbors who need errands and chores done around the house.

3. Finding a mentor

Children do not always accept guidance from their parents. Henske jokes that, "If your name is Mother or Father, that essentially implies that you know nothing until that child turns 30." That is the reason why it is critical to have your children find mentors who can help guide them early on. It could be a local financial specialist, a family friend, or a specialist in their field.

To help clarify their ideas, your children can even create a model or simulation to show local experts, which could prompt accomplishment as it were. Think of something like 'Shark Tank' at a neighborhood level.

4. Researching the market

If you think your child's idea can be a business, first research the market to establish what the need is for it and research the competition. Create a plan of action and, if the idea is a product, figure out the amount it would cost to take it to market.

Don Bossi, the president of FIRST, a non-profit organization that encourages students in grades K-12 to innovate in the fields of science, technology, engineering, and math (STEM), said that if any one of their ideas looks great, children could talk with private investors to check into whether somebody could fund it, taking it from a model and idea to creation and possibly a genuine business.

5. Showing life exercises 'en route'

As you guide your children through building and maintaining their business, talk with them about benefits and expenses. You can also have them read books about celebrated businesspeople.

In any case, do not try too hard. "Don't get caught up," cautioned Henske, "as a parent, trying to use the fire-hose method: You bring the kids in the room one day and sit in the room for five hours and teach them how to be entrepreneurs." I can confirm this from my own experience. Explaining the concept only once is doomed to fail. Success is often achieved by introducing a concept slowly and gradually.

All things must be done one step at a time. The primary concern is often that, if you put in the effort to educate and guide your children, they will absorb your teaching in the long run—maybe slowly, but they'll get there. If we do not show our children to be business visionaries, which involves having an idea and assuming responsibility for their future, they will hold onto their first job and, when it changes or disappears, they will most likely crash without a clear path to move forward. Instead, they will start looking for any available job just to sustain their living.

RECAP

Teaching children to give back is crucial for developing financial literacy and empathy. Use occasions like birthdays to encourage giving to charity instead of just receiving gifts. Involve them in your own charitable activities to demonstrate the importance of sharing with those in need.

Philanthropy is not just for adults or the wealthy. Children can learn that money is less valuable than human connections and community. Simple acts like donating toys can instill a sense of social responsibility and empathy.

To teach giving at different ages, start by discussing community needs with your children, which can inspire them to help. Allow them to choose how they want to give back and establish family giving rituals, such as donating on special occasions. Encourage them to include giving in their budget, even if it's a small amount, to build a habit of generosity.

Financial literacy extends to managing debt and preparing for financial independence. Many young adults face significant debt issues, delaying major life steps due to financial strain. Educating teens about money management, budgeting, and debt is essential. Parents should provide ongoing guidance to help them navigate financial responsibilities and avoid long-term debt.

Entrepreneurship is another vital aspect of financial education. Encourage children to pursue business ideas, no matter how small. Activities like lemonade stands, crafting projects, or app development teach essential skills like planning, saving, and investing. Support their creativity and problem-solving abilities, and help them find mentors and conduct market research.

Overall, instilling the right financial values and encouraging an entrepreneurial spirit prepares children for a financially responsible and independent future. By teaching them to give back, manage money wisely, and explore entrepreneurship, you equip them with the tools to succeed and contribute positively to society.

DIGITAL TRAPS: ENLIGHTENING YOUR CHILDREN

A colleague of mine told me how much his daughter has changed since he canceled his cable subscription. He canceled it because he was tired of watching the same movies and programs all the time. He felt he was not getting the value he was paying for. (So did I! I recently canceled mine and don't miss it!)

Instead, he got other options like Amazon, Disney, Netflix, and other providers. But the thing is, his decision had an unexpected effect on his daughter. She was like many other children, the kind who wants to buy the whole toy store whenever she goes shopping. It wasn't that she did not know what she wanted, it was that she wanted everything she saw on television adverts.

My friend and his wife had been seeking solutions without success. That is, until the cable was canceled. Slowly, and with difficulty, their 12-year-old child began to adjust. It has been four years now since they canceled their cable subscription, and things have changed. She is no longer indecisive, and she has broader interests now beyond Nickelodeon and Disney World. The change was shocking to her parents. After much thought, they stumbled upon the solution: starving her of ads. Sounds simple, right? But it is so true. With the cable canceled and them switching to Netflix, the exposure to ads reduced drastically, triggering other changes.

ADVERTISERS' TRAPS

Over the years, I have done my research and have concluded that advertisers are responsible for a huge part of the financial illiteracy and foolishness we see today in our society, both in children and adults. With the prevalence of advertising and convenient buying options, buyers of all ages are more likely to buy something quickly, whereas they previously may have thought about it a bit more. And this must be clearly addressed if we hope to change it.

Advertisers have gotten sneakier with time with every attempt made to stop them from turning children into zombies. They have adopted different strategies, moving away from the more common and obvious tactics like flashing banner ads, contests, sweepstakes, and even sponsored ads, like the ones you see on Google. Some of the new strategies now are so subtle you might not even realize it's happening, but they do the same thing they were always meant to do.

For example, product owners now turn to media celebrity endorsements. Celebrities are, of course, very willing to play a part in the plan because of what is in it for them: They earn a lot of money marketing products for other people. Tweets and Instagram posts by celebrities about a product also have the same effect, or even stronger, on children, even though social media platforms now clearly label sponsored content, so that people can see it's a brand collaboration.

Children feel pride and joy when they use a product their favorite star is endorsing. It's not just children – many people are proud to be brand ambassadors. They probably don't realize that some of these celebrities do not even use the products they endorse online. The advert is just business for them, and nothing else. They (or their branding team) make their posts and go about their other businesses, while children start looking for ways to get the products no matter what it costs them or how little they need it.

Here is another example: Teens often struggle to cope without their favorite TV shows. So, they might go and sign up for the show's mobile alerts, not knowing that in doing that they have also signed up to receive ads from all the companies partnering with the show. These companies buy your child's details and information, and then use them to send them ads.

Advertisers also adopt other strategies. They now make ads look like games and put them on the web. Which category of people plays online games the most? Children, of course. They use those fake game designs as bait to make children click on the ads and look at products. The effect of this can be immensely powerful.

Advertisers also take advantage of social media platforms like Facebook, making the most of a kid's desire for social acceptance. They do this skillfully, to influence you to want what others think is cool even if they do not need the product. For example, Spotify allows its users to share their listening activities on Facebook, as a way of promoting the platform.

Of course, any innocent child can easily be a victim of all these strategies, unless you protect them from them. Even adults are not safe. One of the ways to give your children protection from social media and TV ads is by teaching your children how advertisements work.

Some younger children, around the age of 7 and below, cannot even tell the difference between an advertisement and entertainment, so they just ingest the ads without thinking. Advertisers are very much aware of this. They know that the earlier children learn about a product, the better the chance that they get their parents to buy it later. Help your kids understand how advertisers plan to trick them. Review ads together and point out the tricks and techniques so your kids can start to spot them themselves.

Also, teach your children about protecting their online privacy. There are sites they should avoid, and they should be careful of the sites and pages they submit their details to online. Children give advertisers lots of information and details to track them; they give out information either by downloading apps or clicking on sweepstakes.

Social media does not help matters with regards to privacy, of course. They may not say it very clearly on their sites, but they are always looking for means to sell their users' behavioral data and make money off them. Never forget however, that a user agrees to this by accepting a platform's Terms & Conditions, although those details are buried in the fine print.

GAMING TRAPS

Recently, I wrote an article about a mother whose son had accidently increased her debt by an unbelievable amount. You might not be that surprised to know how he spent all the money: He spent it on games.

16-year-old Jack took his mother's card out with him when he went out with his friends, and he spent a whole lot of her money playing games and having fun. That was not the first time it had happened. It had happened multiple times in the past and every time the boy felt sorry for weeks but would then go ahead and do it again. The mother loves her son, but she confessed she almost started wondering whether her son might have a gambling addiction or be mentally ill. She couldn't think of any other reason for her son's reckless behavior with money.

I have heard this kind of story before, and I feel unbelievably bad each time because I sincerely think children are unfair victims. They are the financially weak links of the family through whom others can get to the hard-earned money of innocent parents.

If you have witnessed or experienced a similar thing before, you don't need to panic. Most of the time, children are just victims of the psychological maneuvers of game makers. So yes, we can say that a child like Jack was out of his mind when he was spending his mother's money on games, but then again, he was also tricked into it. He was tricked because he was ignorant of the psychological tactics employed by game makers. Maybe if he had been aware of their tricks, he wouldn't have fallen victim to them.

To protect your child properly, you must know some of the strategies used by game owners to make people spend a lot of money on games. Then you can try to help them not to fall into those traps by teaching them these things. Always have in mind that it is your responsibility to educate your children on these issues, especially as it pertains to their finances.

Just like advertisers and product owners, game makers can be sneaky. They try to get into the mind of users, make them form habits or mindsets that will eventually lead them to spend huge amounts on games. Game owners today offer digital products in their games worth tens of thousands of dollars.

If you have ever thought of the reason why children will keep spending huge amounts on a particular game for a long period, then you should know already that the number one and most important rule of game makers is to never run out of content, and they leverage principles from the psychology of addiction to make these things stick. So do advertisers and social media platforms.

Their strategies make their users (your children) keep their business running. Let's just look at some of the strategies they use to keep children running after their content.

The Hook, Habit, and Hobby Loop

Most times, game makers split their plans into steps and make them progressive. The chances that a user will play a game for the first time and immediately spend money on the game is not that high. That's why strategies are often progressive. They keep planting the seeds in their users' minds until they finally spend their money. Often you see that the first version of a game does not have any in-app purchases but, with time, they begin to release updates for the game. The new updates will likely have some major improvements and in-app purchases or services to sell to players.

Game makers do not also expect everybody to freely spend money on the game all at once, so when they get to the stage where they want gamers to spend money, they also come up with strategies to draw people into spending on the games a little at a time at the beginning.

Game makers often use a strategy known as 'hook, habit, and hobby' to draw users into eventually spending big money on their games. Let's review these steps so you can go over them with your child.

The Hook Stage

The hook stage, as the name suggests, is what they use to rope users in. At that stage, a game or app will offer children great and exciting production values; they come up with wonderful graphics and new features that look both very valuable and very cheap at the same time. Before the hook strategy kicks off, they would expect that people have been playing the game for free for some time.

In the free version of a game without in-app purchases, they intentionally create a noticeable need to make the game more engaging. Maybe the graphics will improve, or some new rooms or arenas in the game will make it more interesting. Something that will make users expect an upgrade. It is like suspense in movies. When your child starts talking about a game frequently and the next version or upgrade comes up, just know something might be around the corner waiting to play out.

The game makers finally upgrade or make another version of the game and introduce the hook. The hook is meant to bring unbelievable value while still being cost effective. It is the ice breaker. Users will think that they are being offered a fantastic deal, not knowing that there is a higher price involved, because they buy the hook in return for not just their money, but their attention, time, and ongoing commitment (or addiction). Once they buy into the hook, they become more committed to playing the game. This is where addiction principles come in, which for children could be their first time. If they win or level up, the dopamine hits. This feeling of pleasure in their brain will cause them to seek out more. They will execute all further plans based on this.

The goal of the hook is to create a need and then solve it. That could be to provide players with eye-catching and very transformative upgrades that will make the game more enjoyable and last longer. And by that, they gain acceptance in the mind of users.

It is important at this point to understand that the value conveyed is an illusion. The upgrades become more valuable depending on how well they can create the need and how obvious they make it look to these young players. For example, I played an adventure game once where it was difficult to get enough free coins to upgrade weapons. This made it difficult to kill certain enemies faster.

At the same time, the game creators made the armory room visible, so the players could see the nice weapons in the game, along with their specifications. This leaves players wondering how much more fun the game would be with those weapons. Thus, a need has been born in a very subtle way. The player can already imagine how much better the game will be when they finally fork over the cash to buy the weapons. Then, they pay the game for solving a problem it created in the first place.

Sometimes it is not this straightforward. Game owners are full of tricks. This simple strategy can be well hidden in the game, so much so that you will not be able to figure out their plan. It looks like an innocent upgrade, but it will all have been part of a bigger plan from the beginning.

The Habit Phase

After the hook stage comes to the **habit phase**. Game makers expect that, having passed through the first stage of spending, children should now be more committed to the game. Once the ice is broken, chances are people will pay more as they continue playing.

The habit phase is about progressing through levels and making the game part of one's daily routine. In the first stage, they are selling value out of the needs they have already created. But in this stage, they are selling faster progress. You will be getting new features with premium purchases. This means you may not have to go through a whole lot of stages to unlock a feature in the game, for instance. At this stage, they do not bring indirect upgrades, but they look for ways to make the game more exciting and last longer. Afterall, the last thing they want is for you to get bored and stop playing.

Game makers subtly employ tactics like hard gate passes to prompt players to pay for upgrades or progress. They also use strategies to entice users with shortcuts without hindering their progress in the free sections, ensuring continued interest in the game and avoiding a significant power gap between spenders and non-spenders.

The Hobby Phase

Last on the list is the **hobby phase**. In this phase, players have reached a significant milestone in their game journey. Having progressed through the earlier phases, they have developed a strong affinity for the game and can be considered devoted super fans. These individuals have likely invested in various upgrades and in-app purchases, demonstrating their commitment and willingness to support the game.

To maintain the game's profitability and keep players engaged, developers employ a range of strategic tactics. One such approach involves introducing paid boosters, which offer additional benefits and enhancements to the gameplay experience. These boosters serve as tempting incentives, enticing players to unlock new abilities, access exclusive content, or accelerate their progress within the game.

For instance, in a football game, a paid booster could enable players to expedite the recovery process of their player's health, granting them a competitive edge for a specific game or match. This feature not only adds excitement and variety to the gameplay but also presents players with the opportunity to strategize and optimize their performance.

By incorporating these paid boosters, game makers not only reward and cater to the dedicated fan base but also generate revenue streams that contribute to the ongoing development and maintenance of the game. This approach ensures the longevity and sustainability of the gaming experience, allowing players to continue enjoying and exploring new aspects of the game while supporting the developers' efforts to innovate and expand their offerings.

The Categorization Strategy

Another strategy game makers use to keep selling their content for a long time is **categorization**.

With this strategy, game makers break down monetization into categories. For instance, let's consider a popular mobile racing game. Within this game, the developers offer various categories of monetization, one of which includes shortcuts. These shortcuts can be purchased by players to gain advantages such as unlocking powerful vehicles, accessing exclusive tracks, or acquiring special boosters that enhance their performance.

Suppose two friends are playing this racing game. One friend, due to work commitments, has limited time to play regularly, while the other friend has more leisure time available. Initially, the second friend might have a slight advantage in terms of progress and achievements due to their increased gameplay hours.

However, by leveraging the shortcuts available for purchase, the first friend can bridge the gap and level the playing field. They can invest in a speed booster, which grants them temporary bursts of increased acceleration, enabling them to compete with their friend who has more time to dedicate to the game.

In this way, the shortcuts offered within the game allow players to progress at a similar pace, irrespective of their available playtime. This categorization strategy not only provides a fair and balanced gaming experience but also incentivizes players to invest in these shortcuts to enhance their enjoyment and competitiveness within the game.

The Psychology of Gaming

Now you know how they keep your children spending in games, let us now look at the mind of these game makers and see the psychological strategies they use to persuade your children to buy all their in-game products.

The Hot State – Thinking Fast

I think one of the requirements to become a game maker must surely be to read Daniel Kahneman's *Thinking Fast and Slow*. This book is one of the best books ever written on behavioral psychology, and game makers seem to have all read it, because they use a lot of its concepts.

In his book, Kahneman teaches us that the brain works in two ways:

- the fast way, where we use intuition to prompt quick responses and actions, and,
- the slow way, which involves logical and thoughtful reasoning.

Let us look at the practical implications of this. If I ask you which letter comes before B, you would simply say A without involving a lot of effort or slow thoughtful processes in your brain.

But if I say: "What is the sum of the number of vowels in the alphabet that come before letter M and the number of consonants that come after it?" I do not think you will answer the question effortlessly like you did when it was just about connecting A and B.

In fast thinking, one does not give much thought before responding or acting. One just uses the information stored in their brain to interpret circumstances without going through the proper reasoning process. Game makers try to exploit our fast thinking—no one will start the slow reasoning brain just to make a purchase decision in a mobile game. Children do not give much thought as to whether to purchase a game feature or not, they just make the decisions and start spending the money or make plans on how to get the money to spend on the game.

Game makers know that users do not purchase their in-game features because they have really thought about the purchase and the values. They are selling through the game because, no matter how much value they are offering, nobody will activate the slow reasoning part of their brain for something as small as a mobile game. They try to appeal to a user's fast-thinking brain by making use of instant gratification strategies. This strategy always works.

You do not even need to have played a lot of games to understand how.

Let us assume you download a game app on your phone and, before the start of the game, you were offered a powerful booster. Would you decide to buy the booster in the blink of an eye when you do not need it yet? Even if they are offering it at a discount, you would think about it, engaging your slow thinking brain to determine if it is a good investment.

Game makers do not want to give you this option at just any time, so they wait and offer you boosters when you feel you need them in the game. For example, they make a revive button available immediately after you die in the game, sometimes for a limited time, capitalizing on instant gratification and the heat of the moment.

Loss Aversion and the Endowment Effect

This concept is about the way people value things and what they do for the things they value. I once had the opportunity to teach parents how game makers influence their children and I asked: "Between making a hundred thousand dollars from scratch and keeping a hundred thousand dollars you already have, which will you work harder for?"

Your guess might be right: About three-quarters of the parents in the hall indicated that they would work harder to keep the money or wealth they have acquired already, rather than work to make extra money.

People tend to value maintaining things they already have higher than things they do not have yet. It simply means people value certainty more than uncertainty. Are you familiar with Tony

Robbins' concept of the six basic human needs?[52] If not, I highly recommend it, as you'll understand what I'm trying to say better.

Following Tony Robbins' concept, certainty is tied to our instincts for survival. Games take advantage of the human desire to find certainty by tricking people into buying their in-game products. They give players access to some game features or resources for free, and then take the resources back at some stage of the game or threaten to take it back unless the player meets certain conditions, for example, finishing a level. At the same time, however, they offer players the opportunity to keep the resources they already have by paying for them instead. This works most times because nobody wants to lose or let go of their possessions and they will not want to start from the beginning again.

Again, timing is everything. Game makers know when you might need that extra boost of certainty, so everything is timed accordingly.

Creation of Scarcity

The concept of scarcity works in every market. Customers demand goods and are even willing to pay tremendous amounts of money for the products they want once they become scarce. We all witnessed the panic buying during the COVID-19 pandemic. Toilet paper, pasta—you saw it.

Product owners in every market are very aware of what scarcity does to buying behavior, so sometimes they create scarcity to influence people to buy. You can reflect on the madness people went through in the pandemic to illustrate that.

Game makers also take full advantage of scarcity mindset and, of course, spend a lot of time creating those situations in their games.

To get the picture well, ask your children this question: "How much do you desire rare items in a game?" Game makers create rare items in the game that players desire to get. Your children will do all they can to get these items, even if they must pay a lot for them. The other way they create scarcity and take advantage of players is by creating time-limited offers. This is a great fast thinking and loss aversion technique to make people spend on games.

The Reward Model

Another strategy game makers use on children is the reward model. They create reward systems in the game to catch the attention of players. So, the more they play the more value they get in the game. This makes it easier for them to buy in-game products. Every product will get them closer to the next reward. Buying an extra builder with real money allows you to make progress faster, especially if you log in frequently.

The Hook Cycle Strategy

The value of things is not only tied to how useful they are, but the effort and time put into something increases their value too.

Game makers allow players to create and personalize things in their games. They also use other strategies I already mentioned to get players hooked, because people will spend willingly on things they value. When this happens, the value of the game increases in the mind of the players, and thus they can convince themselves to invest time and money in the game.

Anchoring

This rule is true anywhere and everywhere: When people do not know the price of things, the first suggested price becomes their anchor.

During negotiations, salespeople will usually exaggerate up the price of their products to a certain level. This makes any subsequent negotiation seem more tempting because it deviates favorably from the anchor price and ultimately is closer to what the salesman would originally sell for.

If a salesperson thinks you'll spend a decent amount of money, he'll usually start with his most expensive products first. This is because buying or talking about expensive products will make cheaper products look even cheaper than they are. For example, you would be more willing to pay for a product at $500 if you had just bought another product worth $5,000.

Game makers use this strategy as well. They start by suggesting to players that they should buy expensive features. They however expect that many players will turn down the offer. Then they will follow up with other offers with good discounts, which users are more likely to be willing to pay for, having been exposed to more expensive products.

False Perception

One of the greatest shopping mistakes you will ever make is to go shopping for a new product or go buy a product when you do not know anything about its price range. You might come back already in love with the shop for selling products at the friendliest rate without knowing you have paid twice the amount you should have for that product.

Humans buy products based on the perceived value of them, especially if there's no prices or alternatives to compare. So, if the mall or shop you buy a new product from successfully makes you think highly of the product or makes you perceive the product is of very good quality when you have not used it before, you will automatically believe the product should cost a lot to match the perceived quality. Mind you, product owners and distributors have a lot of strategies up their sleeves to create the perception they want you to have about different products.

Social Proof

Human beings are social animals. We are highly influenced by others, and game makers take advantage of this. You will never catch them announcing to their users that no one is buying their in-game products, but when a few people buy these products, they put a lot of effort into making sure everyone in the group knows about it. Game makers seek to create social norms within the user group that will influence everybody else to spend money in the game.

Ask your child how much he or she spends on games weekly or monthly. Ask casually because, if they feel you are up to something, they might not be sincere about it if they are spending big on games. Chances are they are signed up to a dozen games. When one member of a social group buys an in-game product, they announce it to the whole group, which can, in turn, influence them into doing the same.

The Psychology of Availability

The psychology of availability is like the social proof technique. The concept of availability looks at what people judge to be more likely to happen. The thing is, people judge availability based on what they have been exposed to or hear about more often.

For example, without looking at the statistics, a typical person will estimate that tornadoes kill more people than asthma because tornadoes are always in the news.

However, this estimation is completely wrong because asthma kills twenty times more people than tornadoes do, but I can't remember ever seeing news on someone who died because of asthma.

Game makers are quick to announce to their users and their peers that a member just found a rare item in the game. This makes players look out for and believe they can also get rare items. And once they finally find it, they will willingly part with their money for it.

Strategic Positioning of Core Loops

Game makers set up games in a way to always remind players that the game could be more fun if they bought in-game products. They try as much as possible to make the game store very central to the game. They design the game in such a way that players will go through the store to get to any new loops or stages. The goal is to make players accustomed to the store and with time, make them more likely to buy some of the weapons or tools.

Car racing games use this strategy a lot. Once you are done with a race, it takes you straight to the store to show you possible upgrades you can buy. It also does the same thing before the start of a race.

The Labeling Technique

If you put a label on someone, they are more likely to act according to that label, especially if it is a positive social tag. This is a persuasive technique because humans are social beings and they endeavor to maintain their social status.

Sometimes, game makers intelligently and creatively reinforce labels of generosity and kindness on their players. I think this increases the spending rate in the game. As a parent, for instance, you don't always buy things for your children because you think it is necessary, but because you want them to continue perceiving you as a provider and protector. I'd imagine that's mostly subconscious behavior for most people, rather than something they're fully aware of.

Game makers have their way of putting players under subtle pressure to spend and act according to certain labels.

Competition

This is arguably the biggest reason people spend a lot of money on games. Players want to beat or be better than others in the game. And game makers capitalize on that by creating competition wherever they can. So many games now have online matches or multiplayer options where players from all around the world connect to and play against each other and fight for the top spot.

If a game can create a constant sense of competition between players, players would be very willing to spend lots of money on the game. People in general, and children especially, do not want to be losers at anything. This can lead them to go all out to spend on games to just be able to compete with their friends and other players.

RECAP

We have dived into the impact of digital media on children's behavior, focusing on the tactics used by advertisers and game developers to engage young minds and encourage spending.

Canceling cable and switching to streaming services with fewer ads can significantly reduce your children's exposure to advertisements, leading to more focused and diverse interests. Advertisers play a major role in fostering financial irresponsibility by targeting both you and your children with subtle, pervasive strategies like celebrity endorsements, social media influence, and ads disguised as games. Children, in particular, struggle to distinguish between ads and entertainment, making them especially vulnerable.

To combat this, you should educate your children about the tactics advertisers use and teach them to protect their online privacy. For instance, review ads together and point out the tricks used to manipulate them. Encourage your children to be cautious about the information they share online, as advertisers often use this data for targeted marketing.

Games also employ psychological strategies to encourage spending. One common method is the "hook, habit, and hobby" loop, which progressively engages players and makes them more likely to spend money. Other strategies include creating scarcity, offering rewards, and leveraging social proof. These techniques create a sense of urgency and competition, driving players to make in-game purchases.

Understanding these tactics can help you guide your children to make informed decisions and avoid falling into digital traps. By being aware of the psychological strategies used by advertisers and game developers, you can better protect your children from unnecessary spending and foster financial responsibility.

CONCLUSION

> *The number one problem in today's generation and economy is the lack of financial literacy.*
>
> – Alan Greenspan

In this book, I have tried not only to teach core concepts children should know about money and how to approach them at different ages, but I have also exposed unique threats to today's youth: games and television commercials, which use several psychological principles to make our children spend money unwisely. Almost every child—and many adults, too—has fallen for these tricks one way or the other without knowing it. I took time to elaborate on this so that you will know how to protect your children at home from the traps of advertisers and game owners.

This is most likely the simplest and most comprehensive book you will see on teaching children financial literacy.

I wrote this book because parents often find it difficult to break down the knowledge they have to pass onto their children in a way they will understand. They often wait until their child has grown to start teaching them, but there are a lot of disadvantages to that. To help parents tackle this, I have broken down different lessons for different age ranges to demonstrate how to teach a child of any age to earn, save, spend, invest, and give.

I hope that, having read this book, you will feel empowered to make your children financially sound and responsible. And always remember that's one of the greatest contributions you can make for your child's life.

CONCLUSION

Don't go yet—One last thing to do

If you enjoyed this book or found it useful, I'd be very grateful if you'd post a short review on Amazon, Goodreads, or the platform you usually use to share your experiences.

Your support does make a difference, and I read all the reviews personally so I can get your feedback and make this book even better.

If you're eager to delve deeper into the realm of financial literacy and explore valuable insights for parents, I invite you to visit my blog at www.nuebel.blog. There, you'll discover a wealth of resources, practical tips, and thought-provoking articles that can empower you to guide your children in developing essential financial skills. Together, let's embark on this journey of knowledge and equip our children with the tools they need to thrive in a rapidly evolving financial landscape. Visit my blog today and join our community of like-minded individuals committed to fostering financial literacy in children.

Thanks again for your support!

LITERATURE

Pape, G. (2013). *Money Savvy Children.* Penguin group.

Godfrey, J. (2013). Raising Financially Fit Kids

https://www.ft.com/content/4801084d-41bb-461b-9b92-d9479b07aee3

https://www.cnbc.com/2021/10/13/how-much-debt-each-generation-has-in-the-us.html

https://www.cnbc.com/2018/05/03/sweden-cashless-future-sounds-alarm-bells-for-the-central-bank.html

https://newsroom.mastercard.com/eu/press-releases/232urope-leads-contactless-adoption-as-almost-1-in-2-transactions-are-now-contactless/

https://www.parents.com/parenting/money/family-finances/teaching-kids-value-of-money/

https://www.teenvogue.com/story/credit-card-debt-young-people

https://middleearthnj.org/2018/04/16/debt-load-soaring-among-young-adults-teach-teens-to-avoid-debt/

https://www.parentmap.com/article/more-teens-dealing-with-debt

https://creditcards.lovetoknow.com/Teen_Credit_Card_Debt_ Statistics

2019 National Foundation for Credit Counseling survey statistics

Robert Kiyosaki's Rich Dad Poor Dad, best-selling book

Hopkins, Liza & Brookes, Fiona & Green, Julie. (2013). Books, Bytes and Brains: The Implications of New Knowledge for Children's Early Literacy Learning. Australian Journal of Early Childhood. 38. 23-28. 10.1177/183693911303800105.

https://www.forbes.com/sites/laurashin/2015/04/14/the- money-taboo-why-it-exists-who-it-benefits-and-how-to-navigate-it/?sh=fb7ff872f627

Mastercard 2021 Press Release | https://newsroom.mastercard.com/eu/press-releases/232urope-leads-contactless-adoption-as-almost-1-in-2-transactions-are-now-contactless/

LITERATURE

Amagir, A., Groot, W., Maassen van den Brink, H., & Wilschut, A. (2018). A review of financial-literacy education programs for children and adolescents. Citizenship, Social and Economics Education, 17(1), 56–80.

Danes, S.M. & Dunrud, T. (2005). Children and Money Teaching Children Money Habits for Life. Retrieved from https://www.semanticscholar.org/paper/Children-and-Money-Teaching-Children-Money-Habits-Danes/03510cf9615c281ee134e8471ed97e41aacb8bc3

Hensley, D. (2019, April 29). When it Comes to Money, Practice (and Mistakes) Make Perfect. Retrieved from https://parentology.com/study-when-it-comes-to-money-practice-and-mistakes-make-perfect/

Kobliner, B. (2018, April 5). Money habits are set by age 7. Teach your kids the value of a dollar now. Retrieved from https://www.pbs.org/newshour/economy/making-sense/money-habits-are-set-by-age-7-teach-your-kids-the-value-of-a-dollar-now

Koblinger, B. Make Your Kid a Money Genius (Even if You're Not): A Parents' Guide for Kids 3 to 23. New York: Simon and Schuster, 2017.

LeBaron, A. B., Runyan, S. D., Jorgensen, B. L., Marks, L. D., Li, X., & Hill, E. J. (2019). Practice Makes Perfect: Experiential Learning as a Method for Financial Socialization. Journal of Family Issues, 40(4), 435–463.

University of Arizona. "Parents: To prepare kids financially, give them practice with money." ScienceDaily. ScienceDaily, 27 November 2018. <www.sciencedaily.com/releases/2018/11/181127092523.htm>.

Wellbank, L. (2020, October 1). Best Apps that Teach Kids Personal Finance. Retrieved from https://parentology.com/best-apps-that-teach-kids-personal-finance/

https://financialpost.com/personal-finance/advisers-share-the-lessons-you-should-be-teaching-your-children-about-money

Rudeloff, M. (2018). Der Einfluss informeller Lerngelegenheiten auf die Finanzkompetenz von Lernenden am Ende der Sekundarstufe I. Springer Fachmedien Wiesbaden GmbH

Bödeker, S. (2008). Finanzkompetenz bei Familien fördern – Impulse für die Arbeit im Familienzentrum. LBS-Initiative Junge Familie.

OECD (2020), *PISA 2018 Results (Volume IV): Are Students Smart about Money?*, PISA, OECD Publishing, Paris, https://doi.org/10.1787/48ebd1ba-en.

Fries, K. R., Göbel, P. H., Lange, E. (2007). Teure Jugend: Wie Teenager kompetent mit Geld umgehen. Budrich.

Meier Magistretti, C., & Rabhi-Sidler, S. (2014): Schuldenprävention mit Jugendlichen: das Modell Jugendlohn. Eine retrospektive Evaluation aus Elternsicht. Luzern, Hochschule Luzern.

REFERENCES

[1] Bernath, J., Suter, L., Waller, G., Külling, C., Willemse, I., & Süss, D. (2020). JAMES – Jugend, Aktivitäten, Medien – Erhebung Schweiz. Zürich: Zürcher Hochschule für Angewandte Wissenschaften.

[2] https://www.daysoftheyear.com/days/teach-your-children-to-save-day/

[3] National Foundation for Credit Counseling (2019). 2019 Consumer Financial Literacy Survey. Retrieved January 20, 2020 from https://www.nfcc.org/resources/client-impact-and-research/2019-consumer-financial-literacy-survey/

[4] Next Gen Personal Finance (2022). State of Financial Education Report. Retrieved April 23, 2022 from https://d3f7q2msm2165u.cloudfront.net/aaa-content/user/files/Files/NGPFAnnualReport_2022.pdf

[5] https://www.globalprocessing.com/news/blog/swedens-2023-cashless-goals

[6] https://www.cnbc.com/2018/05/03/sweden-cashless-future-sounds-alarm-bells-for-the-central-bank.html

[7] https://newsroom.mastercard.com/eu/press-releases/europe-leads-contactless-adoption-as-almost-1-in-2-transactions-are-now-contactless/

[8] Kosse, A., & Szemere, R. (2021). Bank for International Settlements (BIS): Covid-19 accelerated the digitalisation of payments. Retrieved December 23, 2021, from https://www.bis.org/statistics/payment_stats/commentary2112.pdf

[9] https://ec.europa.eu/eurostat/statistics-explained/index.php?title=Digital_economy_and_society_statistics_-_households_and_individuals

[10] OECD (2017). "Students' use of ICT outside of school", in PISA 2015 Results (Volume III): Students' Well-Being, OECD Publishing, Paris.

[11] Marsh, Jackie & Plowman, et al. (2015). Exploring Play and Creativity in Pre-Schoolers' Use of Apps: Report for Early Years Practitioners.

[12] OECD (2019). Measuring Distance to the SDG Targets 2019: An Assessment of Where OECD Countries Stand, OECD Publishing, Paris, https://dx.doi.org/10.1787/a8caf3fa-en.

[13] OECD (2017). Starting Strong V: Transitions from Early Childhood Education and Care to Primary Education, Starting Strong, OECD Publishing, Paris, https://dx.doi.org/10.1787/9789264276253-en.

[14] International Telecommunication Union (2018). Measuring the Information Society Report 2018, https://www.itu.int/en/ITU-D/Statistics/Pages/publications/mis2013.aspx.

[15] OC&C Strategy Consultants (2018). Eine Generation ohne Grenzen – Generation Z wird erwachsen, https://www.occstrategy.com/media/1904/eine-generation-ohne-grenzen_.pdf.

[16] Livingstone, S. et al. (2018). In the Digital Home, How Do Parents Support Their Children and Who Supports Them? Parenting for a Digital Future: Survey Report 1, LSE, London.

[17] Chaudron, S., R. Di Gioia and M. Gemo (2018). Young Children (0-8) and Digital Technology, a Qualitative Study Across Europe, European Union, http://dx.doi.org/10.2760/294383.

[18] Marsh, J., Plowman, L., Yamada-Rice, D., Bishop, J., Lahmar, J. and Scott, F. (2018), Play and creativity in young children's use of apps. Br J Educ Technol, 49: 870-882.

[19] Marsh, Jackie & Plowman, et al. (2015). Exploring Play and Creativity in Pre-Schoolers' Use of Apps: Report for Early Years Practitioners.

[20] https://www.abc.net.au/news/2017-08-17/cashless-kids-what-is-tap-and-go-doing-to-the-younger-generation/8812168

[21] https://www.cnbc.com/2021/07/09/have-you-had-the-money-talk-with-your-family-yet-dont-put-it-off.html

[22] https://creditcards.chase.com/slate-edge-credit-card/all-about-credit/having-the-money-talk-with-kids

[23] https://www.troweprice.com/corporate/us/en/press/t--rowe-price---adulting--is-harder-without-any-financial-educat.html

[24] ttps://www.forbes.com/sites/laurashin/2015/04/14/the-money-taboo-why-it-exists-who-it-benefits-and-how-to-navigate-it/

[25] https://www.washingtoninformer.com/conversations-about-personal-finance-more-difficult-than-religion-and-politics-according-to-new-wells-fargo-survey/

REFERENCES

[26] Karen E. Dynan, Jonathan Skinner, and Steve Zeldes. 4/2004. "Do the Rich Save More?" Journal of Political Economy, 112, 2, Pp. 397-444.

[27] http://www.mtmfec.org/many-money-habits-are-set-by-age-7/

[28] McDonough, P. (2009). TV Viewing Among Kids at an Eight-Year High. Retrieved January 29, 2020, from https://cutt.ly/LY5LWlN.

[29] Rideout, V., Foerh, U. G., and Roberts, D.F. (2010). GENERATION M2: Media in the Lives of 8- to 18-Year-Olds. Menlo Park, CA: Kaiser Family Foundation.

[30] Rideout, V., and Robb, M. B. (2019). The Common Sense census: Media use by tweens and teens, 2019. San Francisco, CA: Common Sense Media.

[31] https://www.forbes.com/sites/forbescommunicationscouncil/2019/12/16/why-financial-literacy-in-schools-matters-today-for-the-workforce-of-tomorrow/

[32] Board of Governors of the Federal Reserve System (2019). Report on the Economic Well-Being of U.S. Households in 2018. Washington, DC.

[33] Next Gen Personal Finance (2017). Who has access to financial education in America today? – a nationwide study of 13 million students across 11,000 high schools. Palo Alto, CA.

[34] https://www.irishstatutebook.ie/eli/1996/act/16/ enacted/ en/html

[35] Protection of Young Persons (Employment) Act, 1996.

[36] https://www.redcross.org/take-a-class/babysitting/babysitting-child-care-training/babysitting-certification

[37] https://www.instagram.com/p/CcSwC4TBNEU/? utm_source=ig_web_copy_link

[38] https://www.adultdevelopmentstudy.org/

[39] https://roostermoney.com/pocket-money-chores-list/

[40] https://www.thebalance.com/what-is-the-average-allowance-for-kids-4177812

[41] https://www.cnbc.com/amp/2021/07/28/51percent-of-americans-have-less-than-3-months-worth-of-emergency-savings.html

[42] https://www.bankrate.com/banking/savings/best-worst-cities-for-building-emergency-fund-savings/

[43] Kobliner, B. (2017). Make Your Kid a Money Genius (Even If You're Not). Simon & Schuster.

[44] https://www.cnbc.com/2020/01/29/teaching-teenagers-to-invest-now-will-set-them-up-for-life.html

[45] https://www.morethanmoney.org/

[46] https://www.nbcnews.com/news/us-news/poll-majority-millennials-are-debt-hitting-pause-major-life-events-n862376

[47] https://www.newyorkfed.org/medialibrary/interactives/householdcredit/data/pdf/HHDC_2019Q1.pdf

[48] MORNING CONSULT (2019). National Tracking Poll. Retrieved January 30, 2021, from https://cutt.ly/0Uwfwk2.

[49] https://news.northwesternmutual.com/2019-09-17-U-S-Adults-Hold-An-Average-Of-29-800-In-Personal-Debt-Exclusive-Of-Mortgages

[50] https://www.parentmap.com/article/more-teens-dealing-with-debt

[51] https://www.cnbc.com/2019/09/10/how-to-teach-your-kid-to-think-like-an-entrepreneur.html

[52] https://www.tonyrobbins.com/mind-meaning/do-you-need-to-feel-significant/